CW01501688

Introduction

Dhyan is the source of all things in the Universe, and the sum of all positive energy. Humans are born of this positive energy and go back to it upon death. They are born connected to this source and retain their true nature, 'Ananda', during childhood. As they grow up, they become disconnected from the source due to the distractions of the mind—and this is the primary cause of suffering.

Human suffering, crime, terrorism, pollution and oppression are products of this disconnect from the superpower of 'Dhyan'. If everyone is connected to—and lives in an abundance of—Dhyan, this world will be a beautiful and peaceful place to live in.

As Shri Ramakrishna said, 'He is alone in all forms and formless. He is limitless, and so are the ways to know him.'

DHYAN

DHYAN

Superpower of Man

KARTAR SINGH

RUPA

Published by
Rupa Publications India Pvt. Ltd 2019
7/16, Ansari Road, Daryaganj
New Delhi 110002

Sales centres:
Allahabad Bengaluru Chennai
Hyderabad Jaipur Kathmandu
Kolkata Mumbai

Copyright © Kartar Singh 2019

The views and opinions expressed in this book are the author's own and
the facts are as reported by him which have been verified to the extent
possible, and the publishers are not in any way liable for the same.

All rights reserved.
No part of this publication may be reproduced, transmitted,
or stored in a retrieval system, in any form or by any means,
electronic, mechanical, photocopying, recording or otherwise,
without the prior permission of the publisher.

ISBN: 978-93-5333-509-0

First impression 2019

10 9 8 7 6 5 4 3 2 1

The moral right of the author has been asserted.

Printed Thomson Press India Ltd., Faridabad

This book is sold subject to the condition that it shall not,
by way of trade or otherwise, be lent, resold, hired out, or otherwise
circulated, without the publisher's prior consent, in any form of binding or
cover other than that in which it is published.

Contents

Introduction   *vii*

PART-1
SUPERPOWER OF MAN

1. Ananda   3
2. Dhyan   8
3. Human Science   20
4. Mind and Its Impurities   29
5. Power of Witnessing   35
6. Anhad or Anahad Shabad   41
7. Sahaj Samadhi or Meditation   46
8. Karma and Salvation   55
9. Optimum Living   61

PART-2
FREE YOUR DHYAN TO LIVE
IN PEACE AND ANANDA FOREVER

10. You Are the Whole Universe   73
11. The Universe According to Science   76
12. Universal Interdependence   78
13. The Uniqueness of the Human Body   83
14. We Are Prisoners of Our Minds   89

15. Doing without Doership and Owning
    without Ownership Is the Key   97
16. Nature's Cycle and Cosmic Duality   102
17. How to Raise Dhyan Level   109
18. Living in Present   116

PART-3
YOU ARE THE ONE
YOU ARE LOOKING FOR

19. The Dhyan World   124
20. Matter World   128
21. The Three Planes of Existence and Freedom   133
22. Faith, Destiny, and the Two Types of 'I Am'   138
23 The Body, the Mind, and Dhyan Leakage Control 143
24 Brutal Doership   148
25 From Ananda to Suffering, and Back to Ananda   155
26. Ajapa, or Unconditional Manifestation   160
27. Life Is a Film Displayed on the Screen
    of Space and Time   165

Glossary   **174**

PART-1

SUPERPOWER OF MAN

Ananda

To be human is to be in 'Ananda'. The fundamental nature of human beings is 'Anand Swarup'. Human beings are beyond Joy and Sorrow. When they are in their true nature, they are powerful and effortless in the accomplishment of their tasks. Everything they do is in a state of bliss—in Ananda.

Once, Swami Tulsi Das was asked why he wrote the Ramayana. He replied, 'Sukham'. He meant that there was no reason behind his taking up the seemingly onerous task—he simply wrote it out of Ananda. He did not even make any effort to write it—it was as if everything happened by itself, in Ananda.

When you do something out of Ananda, it becomes perfect. Because in Ananda, you are in your true nature—at complete rest and full of power—and all your senses are free to act.

Our sansar—the material world—is like an ocean. It lies in our mind, restless because of the mind's impurities. If the mind is purified, it comes to rest, and we start truly experiencing our souls. This takes us beyond the material world, allowing us to be at peace during our lifetime and enabling us to join our Creator in the afterlife. The impurities of the mind are distractions that endlessly divide our mind, leading to sorrow. Purifying the mind causes these distractions to end.

The seed of the Bo tree is as small as a grain of sand. In a seed so small, lies a huge Bo tree. We have to sow that seed in a fertile land, water it from time to time, and protect it till it becomes self-sufficient. Then, with time, it will grow up to be as big and beautiful as the tree that provided the seed.

Similarly, a human being is also a seed produced by the Creator of the universe. We have to purify our mind in order to remove distractions and connect it to our soul, which amounts to sowing the seed of consciousness, and then water it by keeping it at rest and away from negative energy. Then, with time, the seed of consciousness will grow into a plant of consciousness and become one with the Creator.

When a human being is born, he or she is connected to the infinite consciousness or soul, because the mind is not yet developed and so there are no distractions. This is why children are in Ananda. But as they grow up and their minds develop, distractions inevitably follow. When these distractions reach their peak with the full development of the mind, the connection to the soul is severed. Impurities fill up the mind, making it restless. This is the beginning of sorrow.

Due to the lack created by this disconnect from the soul, people start chasing after material objects in pursuit of happiness. They start reeling between joy and sorrow in this materialistic world, and get completely detached from the world of Ananda in which they had taken birth.

The main reason for their misery is that they start finding happiness in the material world, which is beyond an individual's control. The more they run after materialistic things, the more miserable they get. They completely forget that their fundamental nature is 'Anand Swarup'.

To be in Ananda one does not need to go out looking for it, work hard, or run after material objects—they simply need to be connected to their own souls, be at rest, be calm, be themselves and stay focused.

King Janak once told his disciples, 'I live in this magnificent palace, but this palace does not live within me. When I am out of this palace, it does not bother me. I am totally detached from it. If I have to leave this palace, I can leave it right now without any remorse. I enjoy all the luxuries of being a king, but I am totally detached from it. It does not affect my inner connectivity in any way.'

There is a beautiful story.

Bodhidharma once visited the Chinese Emperor Wu. The Emperor asked him, 'I have built so many universities and Buddhist monasteries. Please tell me, what merit have I earned?' 'Nothing,' replied Bodhidharma. 'You have not earned anything.' At this, the Emperor was confused. Bodhidharma told him, 'Bragging about one's achievements or proudly displaying what one has done is a manifestation of the ego, which is the source of the negative energy that leads the self to suffering.' The Emperor then requested

Bodhidharma to relieve him of his ego. Bodhidharma asked him to come to the temple where he was staying at three' o' clock in the morning, alone—and told him to bring his ego along.

The Emperor was highly impressed with Bodhidharma's confidence and did not sleep the whole night. He reached the temple at the appointed time, and Bodhidharma was waiting for him. The latter asked the Emperor whether he had brought his ego along with him. At this, the Emperor stayed quiet for some time, before replying, 'Ego is not a material object. It can't be held and taken somewhere. It is inside me.' Bodhidharma said, 'So you agree that the ego is not a thing that is outside. There, 50 per cent of your problem is solved. Now that you feel it inside you, please sit down on that mat and find it. When you find it, please tell me and I will relieve you of it immediately; I am carrying a rod for this purpose.'

The Emperor sat down on the mat and began introspecting. Not being able to find his ego inside, he began trying to tap into his self, conscious of the positive energy all around him—since Bodhidharma, a source of positive energy, was sitting right in front of him. He felt Ananda. He felt relieved of negative energy and became deeply connected to the self. He sat in this manner for one, two, three hours—until the sun began to rise.

Bodhidharma could not wait any longer, and shook him to awaken him. He asked the Emperor whether he had found his ego. The Emperor touched the monk's feet, saying, 'You have truly relieved me of my ego.' 'What happened?', asked

Bodhidharma, to which the Emperor replied, 'There is no ego in reality. It was simply my perception. I dropped my false perception and became relieved of my ego.' At this, Bodhidharma smiled. He told the Emperor that in reality there is no 'I' or 'You', there is only 'He'. When we falsely perceive an 'I', we enter the material world, which is a world of suffering. When 'I' itself is false, then all the relations based on that 'I' are false. 'I' and all its relations collectively make up the material world, which is called 'Sansar'—and 'Sansa' means false. So the whole of the material world, which is composed of the 'I' and its relations, is false.

Realization of this truth can relieve us of our ego. Fear, suspicion, anxiety, guile, hatred, anger, jealousy, lies, cruelty, guilt, duality, greed, etc. are all negative energies, rooted in the ego. The moment we get relieved of such negative energies, we move towards Ananda. This egoless stage is called 'Awakening'.

Raja Janak told his disciple, 'I enjoy all the luxuries of being a king, but never feel that they are "mine"—rather, they are the blessings of my Creator. I enjoy them to realize His blessing, bowing my head before Him in gratitude. I know I only have a limited time to enjoy them, so I do not get attached to them. Whatsoever I enjoy, I always feel free.'

This is the way to be in Ananda.

Dhyan

A blessed master was to address an intellectual audience on the subject of 'Human Science'. He told the audience that he would begin with three questions to help them understand the subject better.

'My first question is, why have you worked so hard since childhood? You worked hard when you were studying in school, then in college, then in university, and now in your profession. Why?'

The replies went, 'I want to lead a happy life', 'I want to serve my country', 'I want to earn more money', 'I want to serve my parents', and so on.

The master summed up the answers and said, 'So what all of you mean is that you have one life, and you want to enjoy it to the fullest, the way you like.' Everyone agreed.

'It is clear that you work hard to enjoy your life to the fullest. Now my second question is, do you really enjoy your life to the fullest?'

The answer was a collective, big 'No'.

The master continued, 'You work hard expecting to enjoy your life, yet you are not enjoying it. There is a big gap. This is the topic for today.

'Why are you not able to enjoy your life to the fullest after working so hard?'

The master went on to explain, 'All of you are moving in the opposite direction. The more you move, the more you get away from your destination. You will never reach it if you continue like this. Real happiness lies within you. The more you run outside and work hard for it, the more you drift away from your real happiness. Your real happiness has nothing to do with your hard work. It depends on how calm you are from within, how centred you are, and how much you are at rest from within. If you are completely at rest inwardly, then you can become so powerful that work no longer seems hard. You can do all work effortlessly and peacefully.

'Work seems hard to you because you are not at peace from within—because you are under stress, under fear of the unknown, under the influence of the negative energy that is consuming your precious energy to make you miserable.'

'My third question is, what is the "superpower" of every human being?'

In reply, the audience mentioned willpower, brain power, patience, compassion, forgiveness, passion, honesty, leadership and more such things.

'You cannot answer the question,' said the master. 'If intelligent people like you do not know the "superpower" of people, what will be the fate of the common masses?

'Dhyan is the "superpower" of human beings. You can also call it attention, awareness, consciousness or soul.

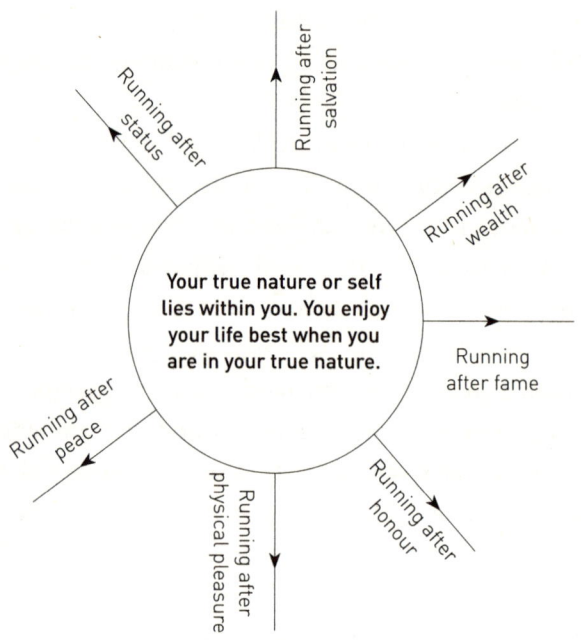

You need not run after these things. You need to settle down in your true nature. Then you will be able to do all these things better, effortlessly and peacefully.

Dhyan is your soul.'

Now you see what you are doing with your superpower of Dhyan. How carelessly you are wasting it. On an average, you are wasting 90 per cent of it and utilizing only 10. You keep on thinking about useless things, which do not need your attention at all. The more you waste your Dhyan, the unhappier you get. To be happy, you must conserve it.

If you analyze the sheer number of things your mind is preoccupied with, you will see how badly your Dhyan energy is leaking, making you miserable. If the leakage increases further, you will go into depression and eventually into deep depression. With further leakage, a person might even be driven to suicide.

On the contrary, if a person has no leakage of Dhyan, he or she is truly happy. If he or she further connects with Super Dhyan—the infinite consciousness—a Ganga of Dhyan flows through him or her, and he or she lives in an abundance of Dhyan, reaching the level of Ananda that is a stage beyond joy and sorrow.

Our mind acts like a bowl. It receives Dhyan from Super Dhyan and distributes it to all the physical senses as per their requirement. Our mind keeps running in so many directions at a time. These directions act like holes in the bowl of the mind, and our superpower of Dhyan keeps leaking through these holes.

Suppose someone has abused you. You immediately take the abuse to heart and keep repeating the person's words in your mind, over and over, while inventing ways to teach him a lesson. You never understand how big a hole it has created in the bowl of your mind, and how much precious Dhyan energy has leaked—and therefore how much happiness you have lost. You could have avoided all of this simply by smiling at the abuser.

Suppose you are deeply attached to your only child, and keep worrying about him or her. This creates a big hole in your mind that keeps on draining your Dhyan energy. More importantly, when you keep worrying that your child may get sick, you are actually exacerbating the chances of the child falling ill, because Dhyan is superpower—it strengthens whatever you concentrate it on. If you continuously and deeply worry about your child falling ill, you are only making it more likely to happen by focusing your energy on it.

Suppose you have a court case and you are constantly worrying about it going against you. By doing so, you are negativity affecting the chances of its going in your favour.

Similarly, if you start a new business and worry continuously about its failure, you are making it more likely to fail.

All your points of deep attachment and hurt create big holes in the bowl of your mind, which continuously keep draining your superpower of Dhyan, thus making you miserable.

Now it is clear that we have unwittingly created numerous holes in the bowls of our minds.

Now suppose you are feeling thirsty. Can you drink water from a sieve?

No, because there are so many holes in the sieve that the water will be drained before it even reaches your mouth.

Similarly, when you want to enjoy something and concentrate your Dhyan on it, you are unable to do so because it is leaking out through all the holes.

Suppose you meet someone you love. If you are leaking Dhyan, this meeting will not make you content. You will keep meeting and leaving discontented, because you are not aware of your leakage. This is how you get addicted—when you continue doing something hoping for contentment, while your Dhyan is still leaking. This is how drunkards, drug addicts, criminals and gamblers are formed—through the leakage of Dhyan.

Now if you plug the holes of a sieve, it will become a bowl and you can drink as much water from it as you like and quench your thirst. Similarly, when your Dhyan leakage is stopped by removing the causes of the holes and by freeing yourself of attachment, then you will be content with whatever you do without becoming addicted. It leaves you free, as you become fully satisfied. The Bhagavat Gita tells us that if you do anything with 100 per cent Dhyan, it becomes Yoga or union with the ultimate consciousness, akin to worship.

Your thinking is powered by the superpower of Dhyan, therefore you become what you think.

You think that your restlessness, fear, anxiety and worries are because of the situation, but they are actually born of low levels of Dhyan within you.

The bowl of the mind, when it is full of holes

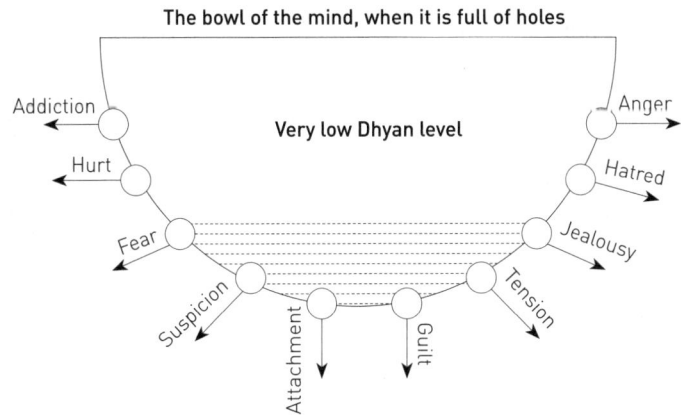

The bowl of the mind, when it is not leaking Dhyan

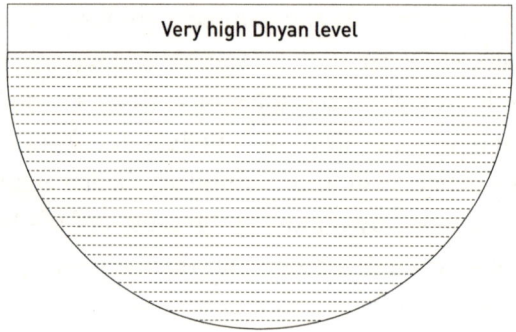

Very high Dhyan level

For further clarification, the master explained,

'Right now, you are looking at me and listening to me. But what happens if your Dhyan is turned off or diverted? You stop seeing and hearing me even when you are staring right at me, with your eyes and ears wide open. You become a statue. After a few seconds, when your Dhyan returns, you return to being a human being and start seeing and hearing me once again.

'What happens to you when your Dhyan is turned off? You become a statue, a mere object. Without Dhyan, your minds and bodies are nothing more than objects. This means that our bodies, and all our senses, require Dhyan to function properly.

'This is true not just for people—animals, birds, insects, and plants are all run by the superpower of Dhyan. And not just living things—in every particle of every non-living thing dances the superpower of Dhyan. That is why it is also called Natraj, or the Dancer. Because it dances within everyone and everything—even the smallest particle of the universe.

'At the level of Dhyan, the whole universe is one. The whole universe is a single dynamic, interdependent unit, and we all belong to it. All things in it are related to each other and dependent on each other.

'Take the sky, for example. We make an earthen pot, but the sky is in it. Take a cup, and the sky is in it; take a room, and it contains the sky. Everywhere, and in everything, we find the sky. And if the pot or the cup breaks, or if we dismantle the room, the sky still remains where it was.

'Similarly, our Dhyan remains where it is even after we are gone. It is the singular, irreducible unit that runs the whole universe. It gives you birth, it sustains your life and it dismantles you in the end for a new beginning, which we call death. This is why we also call it GOD: Generator, Operator and Destroyer (Brahma, Vishnu, and Mahesh).'

The most important characteristic of our superpower, Dhyan, is concentration. It can be concentrated on any subject you want.

If you concentrate your Dhyan on Engineering, you become an engineer. If you concentrate it on the Medical Sciences, you become a doctor. If you concentrate it on sports, you become a sportsperson. If you concentrate it on gambling, you become a gambler. You are where your Dhyan is.

Everyone in your life demands your Dhyan or attention. Your work needs your Dhyan. Your wife, your kids, your parents, your friends, your enemies, your co-workers, your superiors, your juniors, advertisers, TV serials, Facebook, WhatsApp, the Internet—your Dhyan is in great demand.

The reason why WhatsApp, Facebook, Google, etc are valued so highly is that they have attracted a high level of Dhyan in our world.

So now we know that our body and mind are objects, mere materials, and the superpower of Dhyan runs them. There are two types of materials: solid and subtle. Solid materials can be touched and physically sensed: for example, our body is a solid material, as is whatever we experience with our physical senses. Subtle materials cannot be touched, nor seen with physical eyes; these can only be felt or seen with our internal eyes or Dhyan eyes— such as our mind. We can witness our desires, feelings, thoughts and emotions. So these are all subtle materials.

Now, whatever can be observed with external or internal eyes, whether solid or subtle, is still material—an object. But the observer itself cannot be observed, because it is spirit (or consciousness).

The observed is the object, variously called 'material', 'nature', 'Parvati' or 'relative'. And the observer is called 'spirit', 'Dhyan', 'Shiv' or 'absolute'.

Thus,

The spirit penetrates the material to make it function.

Or,

Dhyan penetrates nature to make it function.

Or,

Shiv penetrates Parvati to infuse her with functioning.

Or,

The absolute penetrates the relative to make it function.

This is what we worship in a Shiv Mandir. In the Bhagavat

Gita, Shri Krishna says that he has two powers, 'Apra' and 'Pra'. Pra penetrates Apra to run it. Together they run the whole universe.

There used to be a story for children when I was young. A king had reared a parrot. He got so attached to it and loved it so dearly that his very life force lay in that parrot. It used to fly to the jungles every morning and return to the king in the evening. An enemy of the king came to know of this, and so instead of waging a direct war with the king, he simply began looking for the parrot in the jungles. After several years, he finally managed to capture and kill it, and the king died immediately.

This story would surprise a child, but become patently obvious upon maturity. We all rear our own parrots, whether they be our spouses, children, enemies, jobs, status, fame, property, money, legal cases, or sickness. And we become so attached to these parrots that we leak our Dhyan to the point of being miserable. We need to let all such parrots fly free, in order to be truly happy.

If our Dhyan level is very low, with excessive leakage, then we are living an unhappy life. We live in excessive attachment and fear, which leads to excessive negative energy. We suffer from a brutally inflated ego and restlessness of the mind. We feel separate from the universe. We can become criminals easily, if an appropriate situation arises. We are always ready to go into conflict with others. With further leakage, we can easily move into depression.

So we must attain a high level of our superpower, Dhyan, to always feel God's blessing and lead a happy life.

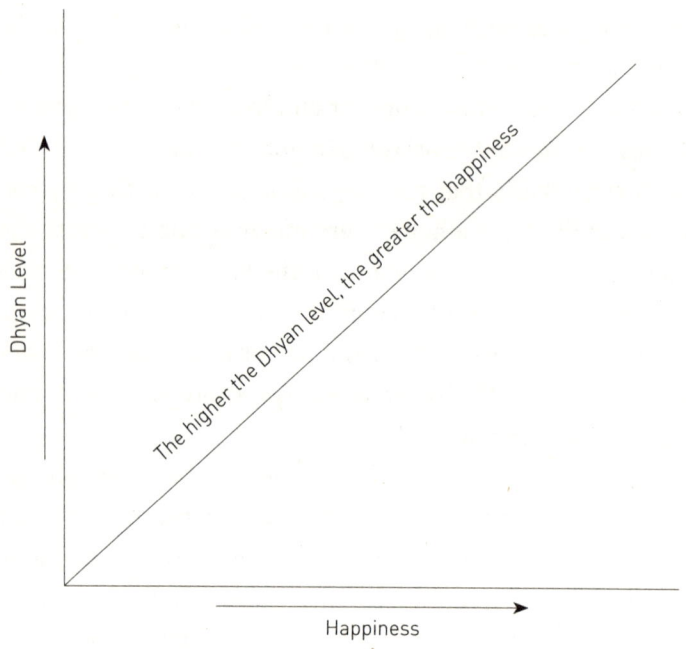

We can concentrate our Dhyan to excel in any subject. America became the world's top economy and superpower by harnessing Dhyan. Lakhs of Americans concentrated their Dhyan energy on research and development. Any country that harnesses the power of Dhyan in such a manner will become powerful. Any person or group of persons—whether they be corporate or social—can become powerful by concentrating Dhyan power, but not necessarily happy. Happiness comes only by connecting with Dhyan or resting in Dhyan. When you connect with Dhyan, you become powerful, happy and wise. Human beings take birth already connected to Dhyan (soul) and are meant to live in an abundance of Dhyan, which is real living. But due to circumstances, they get disconnected and become deficient in Dhyan power—and therefore suffer. All their life, they seek to reconnect.

Human Science

We, as human beings, operate in two different worlds—the material world and the Dhyan world. These worlds are not only different in nature, but totally opposite to each other. The material world is temporary, ever-changing, impure, restless and full of duality and negative energy, while the Dhyan world is permanent, constant, unique, pure, peaceful, eternal and full of positive energy. To live peacefully, we must know how to balance these two worlds.

The Two Worlds and Three Planes of Human Life

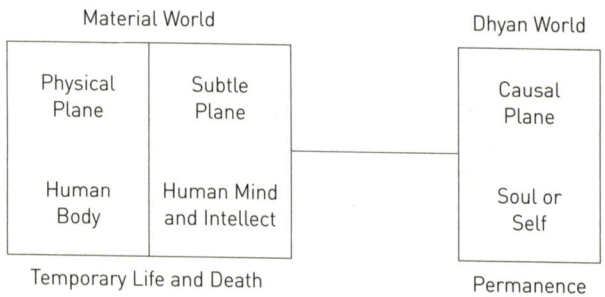

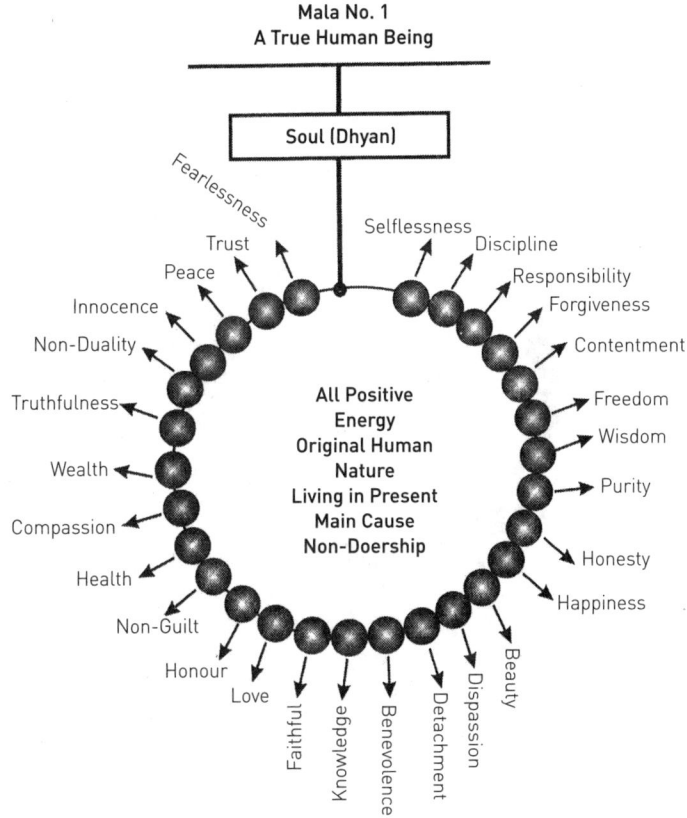

Mala No. 1
A True Human Being

Soul (Dhyan)

Fearlessness
Trust
Peace
Innocence
Non-Duality
Truthfulness
Wealth
Compassion
Health
Non-Guilt
Honour
Love

Selflessness
Discipline
Responsibility
Forgiveness
Contentment
Freedom
Wisdom
Purity
Honesty
Happiness
Beauty
Dispassion
Detachment
Benevolence
Knowledge
Faithful

All Positive
Energy
Original Human
Nature
Living in Present
Main Cause
Non-Doership

When Connected to the Soul (Dhyan World)

When a child is born, he or she is connected only to his or her soul, as the mind does not exist in the beginning. He or she lives in the Dhyan world, as depicted in Mala No. 1. This is why young children are usually so energetic and in Ananda. They emit positive energy. Anyone who comes in contact with them receives this positive energy and becomes happy.

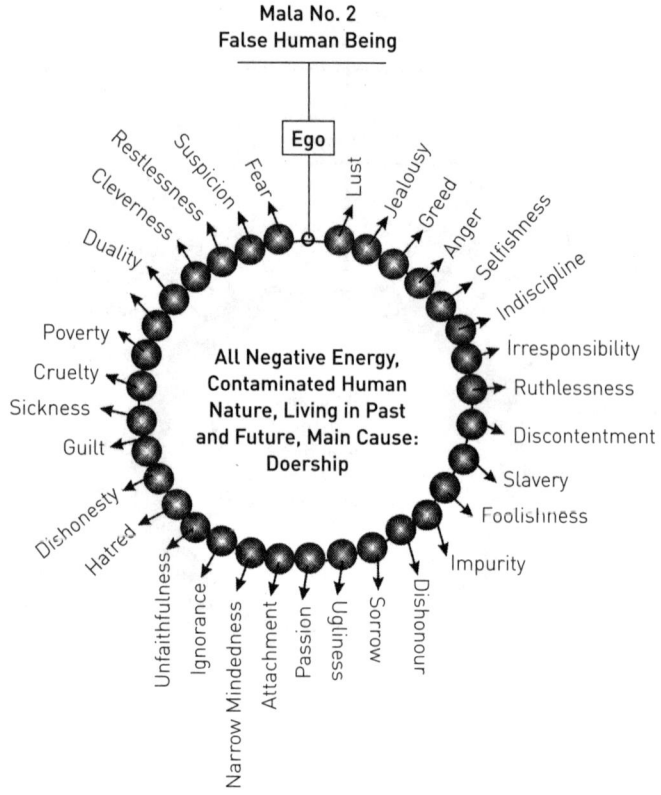

When Disconnected from the Soul (Material World)

As soon as they start growing and recognizing the mother, family members, toys, etc, the contact with the Dhyan world starts weakening. When they reach their teens, the contact is almost fully severed. When they reach adulthood and their natural reproduction cycle starts, the contact breaks completely and they enter the stage of Mala No. 2, that is, the mind world or material world, which is full of negative energy. In adulthood, they become so engrossed in their spouses, children, ageing parents, professions and other responsibilities that the connection to the soul is completely forgotten. Most people die without ever retrieving the contact with their soul—only a few blessed ones are able to recover the forgotten path and awaken once again in Ananda. These people, who are blessed with awakening, again become innocent like children and begin emitting positive energy. They become sources of the positive energy of Dhyan and return to the stage of Mala No. 1, with all its attributes. They thus become free from the cycle of rebirth, as they have freed their Dhyan from the material world full of karma.

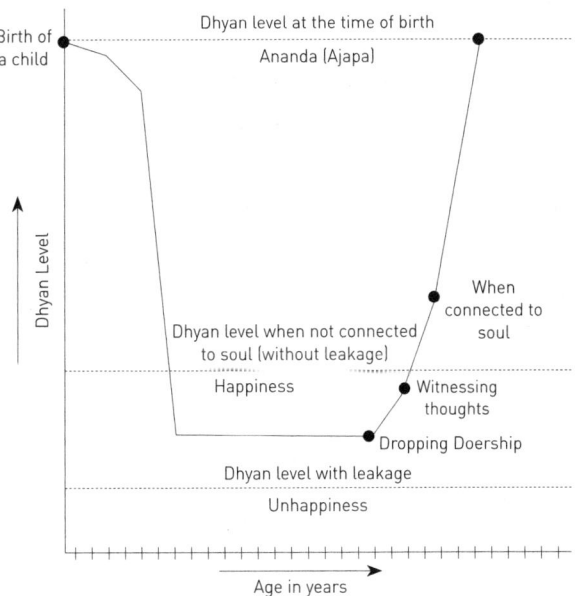

Dhyan level drops drastically after teenage, but can be regained by dropping Doership, witnessing thoughts and connecting with the soul.

These two Malas represent the two worlds in which a human being exists. Mala No. 1 belongs to the Dhyan world and Mala No. 2, to the material world. The threads of these malas represent the powers on which all the beads, which signify the attributes of human beings, rest.

Mala No. 1, belonging to the Dhyan world, bears the thread of soul (Dhyan) and carries the beads of positive energy.

Mala No. 2, belonging to the material world, bears the thread of ego and carries beads of negative energy.

All human attributes, positive or negative, rest on a single factor in each of these worlds. In Mala No. 1, it is the soul, and in Mala No. 2, it is the ego. In both cases, if the thread is broken, all the beads will scatter.

If the thread is broken in Mala No. 1, indicating that your contact with your soul is broken, then the beads of positive energy are scattered and you enter into Mala No. 2, which is the stage almost all adults share.

Now in Mala No. 2, the thread is that of ego, and all the beads are of negative energy. Our superpower of Dhyan is being drained badly because of this negative energy, making our lives miserable in turn.

But now we know that we can kill all of our negative energy in one stroke by breaking the thread of Mala No. 2, which is ego. As soon as the thread of ego breaks, all the beads of negative energy will be scattered in one stroke.

Now, to destroy ego we will have to destroy its roots, otherwise it will crop up again. The root of the ego lies in 'Doership'. We will have to destroy this Doership in order to eliminate negative energy.

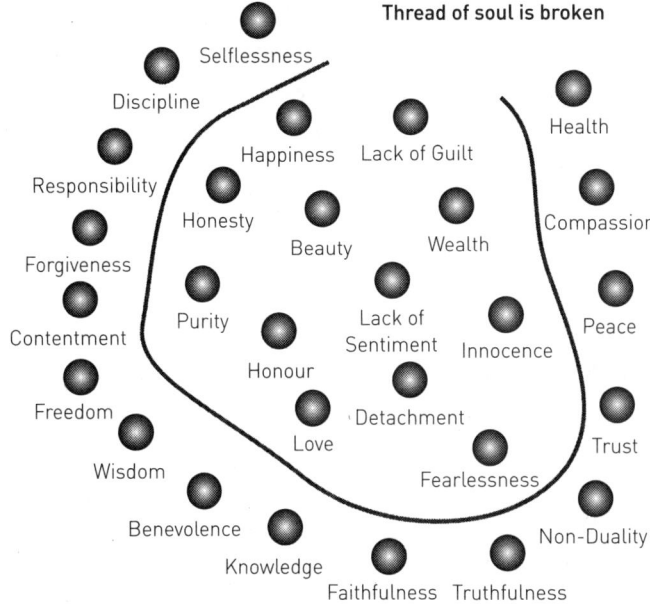

When all beads of positive energy are scattered, human enters Mala No. 2

What is Doership?

All the emotions, worries and restlessness that affect you while taking an action constitute 'Doership'. You think you are the 'Doer' of the action, and if you don't do it, it will not be done. In reality, you are not the Doer—it is Nature that is taking every action through you, thereby making you a 'non-Doer'. You do not own the action—you are only an agent through whom something is being done. If you are able to settle in peace within yourself, with your soul, then you abandon Doership or ownership of action, and become a non-Doer. Upon abandoning Doership, you will realize that you had been wasting your Dhyan energy in emotions, worry and restlessness, and that had been making you weak. Now the same Dhyan energy can be saved and can help you perform the same actions effortlessly, while remaining peaceful and happy.

Non-Doership removes all negative energies attached to the action, and the energy thus saved makes you so powerful, efficient, peaceful and happy that the action becomes effortless.

In the Gita, Shri Krishna told Arjun, 'You are not a Doer. Do your duty which comes your way naturally and earnestly.' Shri Krishna further listed:

1. Do not get emotionally involved in the action.
2. Do not worry about the success or failure of the action.
3. Do not worry about the fruits of the action.

All of the above mentioned points belong to Doership. Now why should these not be done?

1. When you get emotionally involved in the action, 25 per cent of your Dhyan gets leaked into it.
2. When you worry about the outcome of the action, 25 per cent of your Dhyan again gets leaked.
3. When you worry about the fruits of the action, another 25 per cent of your Dhyan gets leaked.

As you can see, 75 per cent of your Dhyan has already been leaked even before performing the action, and you are left to perform it with only the remaining 25 per cent.

The probability of success is thus limited to that 25 per cent and the probability of failure is close to 75 per cent. This is how your Doership affects your actions. You are the reason for your own failure and you become filled with tension, worry and restlessness.

If you are at peace and at rest from within, you perform all your actions with 100 per cent Dhyan. Then it becomes effortless. It increases your efficiency and the quality of your work, and improves relations all around.

The thread of ego is broken

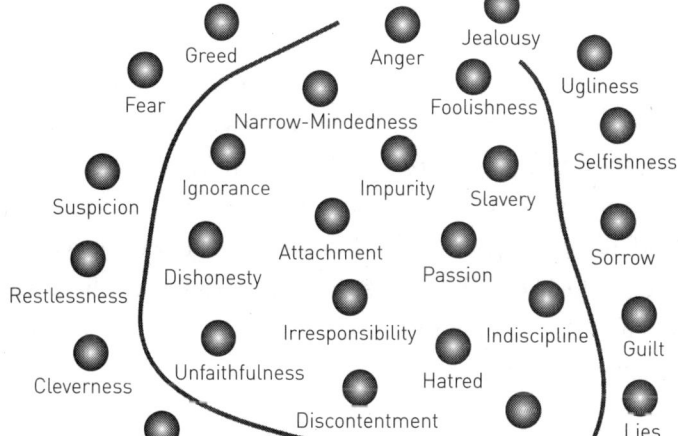

When all beads of negative energy are scattered,
a human enters Mala No. 1

Now we have successfully come out of Doership and dropped our ego. Thus the thread of Mala No. 2 has been broken and the beads of negative energy have been scattered in all directions. In one stroke, we have freed ourselves from the negative energies that affect our actions.

Let us take the example of water. If we water dry grass, it turns green. Because water is the life force of the grass. If we add poisonous chemicals to the water before watering the grass, however, the grass will go dry—the exact opposite of its true nature. This is because we have added impurities to it. Similarly, all the negative energy of Mala No. 2 acts like poisonous chemicals that affect our humanity. Our original nature is all positive energy. The negative energy is the outside element. The very same human being who was to bring peace and harmony to society is doing the exact opposite—bringing unrest and conflict. This is all because of the influence of the outside element—negative energy.

If we want peace and harmony in the world, we will have to flush out the negative energy from ourselves, and therefore from humanity. Then, there will be peace and happiness all around.

Mind and Its Impurities

All children are born alike, with the same godly powers, but the karma resulting from their experiences and influences leads to a blockage of Dhyan energy. Since children are impressionable, this restricts their growth and human potential. Children most often receive these blockages from their parents, friends, teachers and society.

Suppose a child's parents are superstitious. When this child grows up, he or she will also be superstitious, which will act as a blockage to his or her growth.

In some societies, women cover their faces and are not free to go outside alone. This becomes a block in the free flow of their Dhyan energy, and therefore to their growth.

Should a child's parents be liars, the child will also pick up the habit, and it will become a block in his growth.

When a child is growing, whatever it observes around it becomes a part of its subconscious mind or memory, and it reproduces the same upon reaching adulthood. When these influences are negative, they act as blocks in his growth.

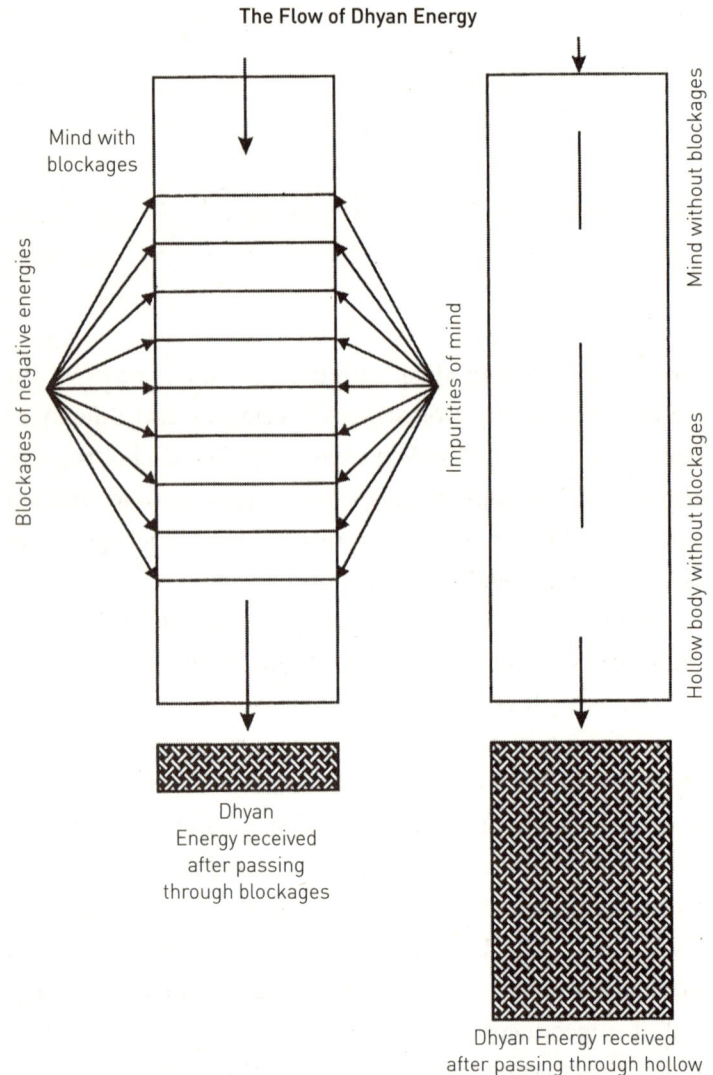

The Flow of Dhyan Energy

The superpower of Dhyan is very weak in blocked minds and very strong in unblocked ones.

Our mind is just like a computer. Just as data is fed to a computer's memory through ports, data is feed to our minds through our ten senses. Similarly, they cannot reproduce data that has not been fed to their memories. A computer cannot reproduce HR-specific data if it has only been fed accounts-specific data; similarly, someone who has never been taught English cannot speak it if asked to.

Everything we take in through our senses enters our subconscious mind or memory. This mixture of good and bad impressions from our past is called karma.

These past impressions, lying dormant in our subconscious minds, keep creating a subtle pressure that prompts us to do certain things and prevents us from doing others. For example, if you enjoyed something in the past, then the memory of that event in your subconscious mind will pressurize you into seeking out the same opportunity over and over again. This may create addiction. Similarly, the memory of a bad experience will pressurize you into avoiding similar experiences. These past impressions lying in our subconscious minds are responsible for our desires, likes and dislikes, addictions, repulsions and the entirety of our behaviours.

Our Vedas, and other holy books, have given a high level of importance to the development of the human mind. All of education, training and traditions are used for this purpose.

The mind is like a clean mirror, and all past impressions, good or bad, preserved in memory are subtle materials. They stick to the clean surface of the mind and make it dull. These are called impurities. As we see everything and everyone reflected through the mirror of our mind, we misjudge them because the surface of the mirror is dull or distorted and therefore unable to reflect the true image. Our misjudgements lead to bad decisions and worse results. Bad results give rise to restlessness.

It is not possible to clean these impurities one by one, because they are unlimited. For this we will have to break the thread of ego, which is the root cause of all these impurities, to clean our mind mirrors. And for this, we need to understand that we are not Doers.

All actions are taken by our body, mind, and senses, which are part of Nature. Our soul, or Dhyan, which penetrates Nature to run it, is a non-Doer. 'We' are souls, not bodies and minds. The soul is pure, non-changing, eternal, restful, bright, innocent, all-powerful, self-aware, sentient, and free of birth and death. As our true nature is soul, we are in our true nature when we are at rest from within— when we get connected to our souls the mirror of our mind becomes clean. Because when we are at rest, no material impurity comes into action. Now everyone and everything will be properly reflected in our mind mirrors, allowing us to judge them properly and make correct decisions. This will lead to good results, and consequently, our minds will be freed from restlessness and can then be at peace.

Master Rinzai of the Rinzai school of Buddhism said that the mind has no definite form—it runs through the whole universe. It acts through various sensory and motor organs freely, because it has no definite form of its own.

Some Zen teachers have described the universe as one mind that expresses itself in many different forms. They say when someone is enlightened, his or her own individual mind reaches this fundamental level of the One mind.

Friedrich Schelling, the German philosopher, wrote that the mind sleeps in the stone, dreams in the plant, awakens in the animal and becomes conscious in man. So the mind is already inherent in each particle of the universe.

Everyone, everything and every particle gets the illumination of consciousness through the mind, which means the degree of consciousness depends on the receptivity of the mind. When the human mind is purified, it becomes highly receptive to consciousness and, thus, enlightened.

You suffer because of lack of self-control. But if you don't know about the self, how can you have self-control?

The Gita says the human body is superior to other materials, that senses are superior to the body, that the mind is superior to the senses, that intellect is superior to the mind and that the self (soul) is superior to intellect. Once we shed our ego, our mind comes to rest and we experience our self. We come to know that this self is all-powerful — that it owns everything and runs the whole universe. We can control our intellect, which controls the mind, which further controls the senses, which ultimately controls the body. This is how we can win control over our mind. In this manner, self-control is won. The mind that was controlling you and causing suffering comes under the control of your self. This self-control is the key to your happiness.

Kabir said:

Kabir Mann Nirmal Bhaia
Jaise Ganga Neer,
Pache Laago Har Phire,
Kahet Kabir Kabir.

(My mind has become pure like the water of the Ganges. Now the creator runs after me calling, 'Kabir, Kabir.')

The ultimate task is to purify the mind to the highest level. Everything else will fall in line.

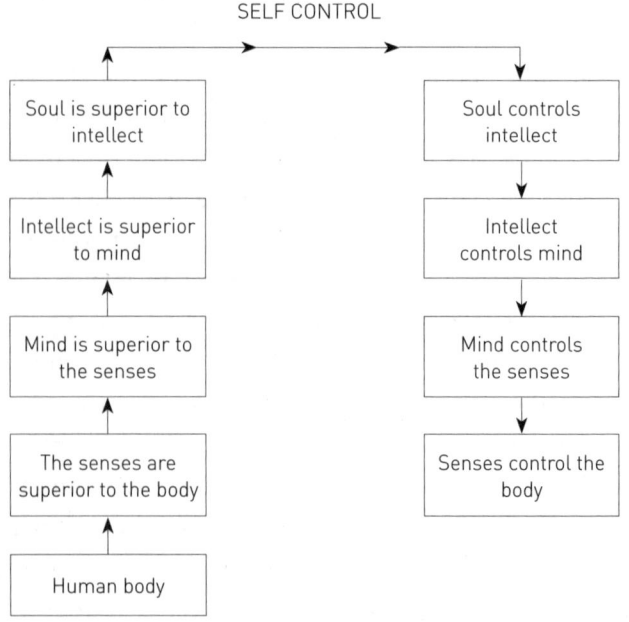

You need to connect to the self (soul) for self-control

Power of Witnessing

The superpower of Dhyan is your Creator, as well as that of the whole universe. He is the only witnessing power, as He is present in each and every particle of the universe. He is the sole witness of each and every thing. It is He who sees through everyone's eyes. Without Dhyan, no one can see anything. It is He alone who is the power behind all your senses. Without Dhyan power, we are simply a statue of matter.

At present, our all-powerful witness is influenced by nature or the material world. He is busy in witnessing the beauty of the material world and living a life of joy and sorrow and bondage. If persuaded, the same witness can witness the negative energy and thoughts in your mind and purify it. The purified mind then comes to rest and you escape the bondage of material world.

Our mind behaves just like a child. A child sees his mother cutting vegetables in the kitchen with a knife. He tries to hold the knife and do the same thing. His mother stops him, afraid that he may cut himself. Similarly, the child tries to jump down the stairs and the mother stops him, fearing that he may break his leg. The mother knows that the child is ignorant—he does not know what he is doing, because his reasoning has not yet developed. When the mother is asleep, the child will indulge in all of these forbidden things, and end up being hurt in the process. Similarly, the mother inside you is asleep and your mind is doing whatever it wants without anticipating the repercussions. This 'mother inside' is called a witness. If we are able to awaken a witness inside, it will take care of our mind and stop it from doing negative things.

What is a witness?

Suppose your friend comes to you and asks for your car in an emergency—perhaps his child is sick and he does not have the transport. You refuse, since you need the car to go to an important meeting. Yet a voice inside you says, 'Why are you not helping him? He has helped you so many times. His child is ill. You can reschedule the meeting.' Swayed by this inner voice, you call your friend and hand over your car to him immediately, earning his thanks.

This inside voice is the witness. We all have witnesses inside, but they wake up only in emergencies.

We need to awaken this witness on an all-time basis. This can be easily done. You will have to be conscious in the beginning, but slowly, when you come to realize that most of your problems are being solved by this witness and your happiness grows and becomes constant, the witness automatically becomes active round the clock.

Your Dhyan is very powerful. Suppose you are driving a car. Your attention is on the steering wheel, but you also look in the side mirrors and the rear-view mirror, and you are talking to the co-passenger as well. If somebody suudenly appears in front of your car, you apply the brakes. You can do so many tasks simultaneously. Similarly, a portion of Dhyan is awake inside you as a witness, to keep a check on the movements of the mind. This witness takes care of the negative actions of the mind as well as the negative thoughts.

Mother Nature gives us everything in raw form. We have to treat whatever she gives us in order to make it suitable for human consumption. We treat the grains—we wash, dry, grind and cook them before consuming. We treat the fruits—we wash them and cut them before eating them. We treat vegetables similarly; we filter water before drinking. We filter out foul or smoky air by keeping a cloth over our mouths or noses. But we do not treat the most important thing that Nature has given us—thought. We consume all our thoughts, good or bad, as they come. We have no system to make them suitable for human consumption. This is the main reason for our suffering. Negative thoughts create negative energy, which eats away our positive energy—Dhyan energy—making our lives unhappy. Our witness is meant to work as a filter for our thoughts, to make them suitable for human consumption. All negative thoughts, when witnessed, are finished.

You cannot 'push' darkness out of a dark room, because darkness is not actually a material thing—it is the absence of light. If you bring light to the room, the darkness will leave automatically.

Similarly, negative thoughts signify a deficiency of Dhyan. You need to inject Dhyan into your mind to quell negative thoughts. Our witness is Dhyan itself. That is why when we witness our negative thoughts, they are finished. We can witness our negative thoughts to filter out the negativity from entering our subconscious minds. Slowly, our minds start becoming pure, and when they are completely purified, they come to rest.

In Hindu mythology, the 'trishul' is a very powerful weapon used to kill demons. The witness is a trishul. It kills the demons of negative energy in thought.

Suppose you are angry for some reason. If you witness your anger, then three things will be finished at the same time:

1. Your anger
2. The reason for your anger
3. Your witness

That is why the trishul has three edges, indicating that three things are finished at a time.

In Sikhism, one of the five signs is the 'comb', which is a holy sign meant to symbolize the cleaning of hair. But it also indicates that someone who strives to be pure should clean their inner thoughts in the same way they clean their hair. It is also a witness.

A witness is a very powerful tool to eradicate negative energy at the stage of thought, and filter it out before it enters our subconscious mind and gives birth to negative karmas.

Our soul is a witness. Our soul is all positive energy, and when we witness something, we inject that positive energy into the thing. If we are able to witness our actions and thoughts, negative energy cannot form—because, as stated above, negative energy is merely a deficiency of positive energy.

Ashtavakra said to Raja Janak, 'Leave your body and rest in Dhyan and be a witness. By doing this, you will become free while still alive.'

A king once asked the Buddha, 'Why do all your monks have faces that are so peaceful, graceful and bright, while everyone else looks sorrowful?' Buddha told the king that his monks live in the present. They do not leak their precious energy and remain full of positive energy, while others keep hopping between the past and the future, due to which they leak their precious energy of Dhyan and lose their charm. To be in the present, you have to be a witness. In the present, there is no leakage of Dhyan energy.

It is very important to know the difference between 'witness' and 'onlooker'. When your Dhyan looks through your mind or your ego, it becomes an onlooker, whereas when the same Dhyan looks through your soul, without ego, it becomes a witness.

As stated before, Dhyan has a natural property—it can be concentrated on anything. When it is concentrated effectively, the Dhyan level rises and one gets greater clarity about the object it is concentrated on.

People who have concentrated their Dhyan on a particular subject and succeeded in achieving high positions in society are often not able to take full advantage of their success. This is because when they concentrate, although their Dhyan level rises, along with it rises the level of the false 'I am' or ego—which eclipses the entire brightness or power of their Dhyan. They remain ignorant about this. This ignorance turns them into arrogant and egoistic persons, and their Dhyan power turns into negative energy—which, as stated above, is a deficiency of Dhyan energy. This narrows their vision and makes them greedy and selfish. This badly affects their peace, harmony and real prosperity, along with those of all the people connected to them.

At this position, if they are able to witness their false 'I am' or ego effectively, it will vanish, as this ego is imaginary, not real. They will come out of the eclipse of negative energy and will begin to shine brightly in the positive energy of Dhyan, which will result in great prosperity, harmony and peace everywhere.

Anhad or Anahad Shabad

Anhad Shabad is the name of the Creator of the Universe. He is beyond human languages and words. He is beyond the reach of the human body and mind. He is the Creator himself. He is your soul, or Dhyan. You can experience him only through your Dhyan. He is also called the voice of silence, the cosmic music or the cosmic sound.

Every sound we hear in this physical world has a particular boundary, beyond which we cannot hear it. Even the biggest explosion will not be heard beyond a few thousand kilometres. But Anhad Shabad is everywhere. There is no space where Anhad Shabad is not present. It is present in each and every particle of the Universe. That is why we call it Anhad, which means beyond boundaries, beyond limits.

Every physical sound in the universe is produced by friction between two or more things. There cannot be any sound without friction. We speak due to the friction between our throats, tongues and air. This friction is called 'Ahat'. Anhad Shabad is also called 'Anahat', which means produced without friction. Anhad, or Anahad Shabad, happens automatically without any friction. That is why it is also called Anahat Shabad. Both of these attributes—that He is beyond limits and beyond material friction—show that He belongs to the Dhyan world.

We were connected to Anhad Shabad when we were born. As we grew and began recognizing the material world, the connection started breaking. Upon reaching adulthood, we completely forgot Anhad Shabad and and turned into false people. We entered the material world of joy, sorrow and bondage, and forgot our real world of Ananda.

Here we call it 'sound' or 'music' in order to create an easy point of reference for those who are enraptured in the material world, as they will only understand such material referents. In reality, Anahad Shabad is neither a sound nor music. Nor can you hear it. It is the presence of the Creator of the universe. It is the presence of our soul. It is Ananda or rest. We cannot hear it because it is beyond the physical world, beyond the body, the mind and the senses. You can experience it only through Dhyan. And you can experience it because your self is also Dhyan. It is your being. You simply need a person who has already experienced it to connect you to it.

When you rest in Anhad Shabad, you rest in the present moment. You settle in your original nature, which is Ananda. You realize that you are a soul, that you belong to the Dhyan world, not this physical world. And you also come to know that you are beyond birth and death, and a non-Doer.

However, although the whole universe is run by Anhad Shabad, the latter never involves itself with it. It always remains a non-Doer, like the sky. The sky never sticks to anything in spite of being present everywhere and in everything.

The Gita says that our soul, Dhyan or Anhad cannot be cut by any weapon, burnt by fire, made wet by water or dried by the wind.

Whatever we see happening around us—children playing, birds chirping, plants growing, animals grazing, men and women working, stars moving, seasons changing, the sun and the moon rising and setting—has a Creator behind it. This is Anhad Shabad working in the universe. It is He who resides in everything and every activity. He, alone—none other.

Human beings are always eager to connect to their superpower, but they do not know it. If we count the investments made on places of worship, holy books and other activities in this regard across the world, we may arrive at the largest sum in the history of mankind. These investments are made simply to reconnect human beings to their Creator, and turn them, once again, into real human beings.

There are a lot of holy books that narrate the experiences of sacred people, written in the form of songs to touch the human soul. But instead of following these books, human beings are busy in simply reciting them. There are some exceptions who follow these books and the teachings of these sacred people, and they are able to transcend this physical world. Our words and languages are inadequate for expressing their contribution to human society. We can only bow our heads in gratitude.

Generally, places of worship have two things in common—sound and light. We go to temples and see bells and lamps. In Gurudwaras, we find Garyaals or Nagaras for sound and lamps for light. In churches, there are organs and candles; in Buddhist monasteries, drums and lamps.

All places of worship are manmade and therefore symbolic or indicative. They indicate that the human body is the real temple of God. Go inside your body, and find sound and light within. This sound and this light represent the Anhad Shabad. Anhad Shabad has a sound and it is luminescent—it has a light of its own. When you get connected to this sound and light, you get connected to Anhad Shabad, or your soul, or Dhyan, or the Creator of the universe—whatever you choose to call it. Upon being connected, you start resting in it. This is the same as resting in your soul or in your being. Now you become a real human being, as you were when you were born. Now you have transcended the physical world of materials, and entered the Dhyan world, which has been represented by Mala No. 1 in Chapter 3.

For more clarity on the Dhyan world or mind world, refer to the following chart:

Dhyan World	Material World
Connected to Anhad Shabad	Disconnected from Anhad Shabad
1. Atman	Mind
2. Superpower of Dhyan (The Creator itself, or Shiv)	Nature or Parvati or material world

3.	All positive energy	All negative energy
4.	Pure	Impure
5.	Eternal	Decaying
6.	Peaceful	Restless
7.	Self-shining	Full of darkness
8.	Without form	With and without form; solid and subtle
9.	Without distractions	Full of distractions
10.	Without ego	Full of ego
11.	Non-Doer	Full of Doership
12.	Without birth and death	Cause of birth and death
13.	Constant without any change	Always changing
14.	Free from bondage	Trapped in bondage
15.	In present (always)	In past and future (always)
16.	Original human nature	Contaminated human nature
17.	Oneness with the universe	Living in duality as independent
18.	Ananda world	World of joy and sorrow
19.	Optimum living	Lowest level of living

From the above, it is clear that if you want to live in your original nature, in an abundance of positive energy and Ananda, you must connect yourself to Anhad Shabad and lead an optimum life in the 'present'.

Sahaj Samadhi or Meditation

We are completely lost in the rush of physical life and have forgotten the path to our self. The path that connects to the Divine, the Truth and the Creator. The path to Ananda. When we were born, we knew this path, but as we grew older, our tendencies and mental distractions disconnected us from it. The revival of this connection to the self is called Sahaj Samadhi or Meditation. Sahaj means 'at rest'. When our mind is at complete rest, we can easily connect to our soul.

Ashtavakra has said that while you may dream when you close your eyes at night, your life is also an open-eyed dream. It is a little longer, but it is still a dream—because we do not know the true reality. Only when you get connected to your soul do you come to know the reality. You also realize that your life, as perceived through the mind, is a dream. Connecting to the soul is called awakening. The awakened life is the real life. Once you awaken, you know that the physical life is temporary. Then you stop rearing parrots and are able to detach easily. Detachment is the only way to come out of this dream world. You also come to realize that the Dhyan world is the only real world. It is where we come from and it is where we have to go. In the Dhyan world, there is no Doership and no death.

Our soul is the ultimate truth. It is the source of our lives. It is the universe itself. We are one with the universe; we are not alone. We are interdependent, not independent. Our suffering only began when we became disconnected from the universe because of our ego.

To reconnect with our soul we have to cleanse our mind of all impurities, so that it comes to rest. This can be done in three ways.

1. (a) Correcting our perception of I to feeling oneness with the universe. When we feel one with the universe, the 'I' vanishes and all the negative energy produced by 'I' also vanishes.

    (b) Dropping Doership and establishing Non-Doership.

    (c) Witnessing thoughts. When we witness our thoughts, negative thoughts disappear and they do not enter our memory. When we establish ourselves as mentioned above, our minds become purified and come to rest. We can then easily connect to our souls with the help of someone who is already connected.

2. We can start verbally chanting the holy name of whichever version of the Creator is dearest to us. Chanting has four stages.

    (a) We chant and a person sitting beside us listens.

(b) We chant so quietly that the person sitting beside us cannot hear us—only we can.

(c) Even we cannot hear it; we witness the chanting happening inside us. In this stage, we can connect to the soul with the help of a guide.

(d) The fourth stage is Ajapa, or auto reciting, which shall be explained below.

3.   Our mind is directly influenced by our breathing. When we are angry, our breathing runs faster than when we are calm. Taking advantage of this factor, we can empty our minds temporarily with breathing exercises. Our empty minds come to rest and we easily get connected to our soul. The human body has seven energy centres. To cleanse the mind properly, we must divide them into three parts and exhale with a little force from these places:

(a) Between lowest end of the spine and the navel.

(b) Between the heart and the navel.

(c) Slightly above the forehead.

This process must be repeated forty to fifty times, in the order of a>b>c. Take the help of an experienced person for this.

By performing this breathing exercise, our empty, restful mind can get connected to Anhad Shabad, or our souls. Try to listen to the cosmic sound, which various saints have described differently according to their experiences. Kabir compared it to the sound of the rain. Other saints have compared it variously with the sound of wind, that of beetles, and that of musical instruments like the flute or ringing bells.

Now that you rest in this sound, you can experience your soul; as this sound is the soul. The mind is halted temporarily. By experiencing it again and again, your connection with the soul is strengthened and your mind is increasingly purified. When the mind is fully purified, your connection with the soul is established.

When you remain in meditation for a long time, the path is cleared and you start hearing the sound round the clock. This is called 'Ajapa'. It is the automatic recitation of the sound, also known as auto-recitation. This stage is similar to the stage when you were born.

Guru Nanak openly declared, '*Nam Khumari Nanka Chari Rahe Din Rat* (I am enjoying the intoxication of the Creator's Name day and night).'

Hazrat Mohamad Sahib listened to this sound in a cave for six years. He said, 'I can hear his sound all the time, but your ears are not blessed.'

Bodhidharma sat facing a wall and listened to the sound for nine years.

Jesus Christ said, 'Know the Truth and it will set you free.'

The Gita says, 'The soul is the only Truth. Everything else is false and decaying.' It further says, 'Perpetual rest in the soul is the end of the quest for truth. It is the only knowledge, everything else is ignorance. It is the only wisdom.'

Buddha's last words were, 'All composite things decay. Work out your salvation with diligence.'

Shri Guru Arjun Dev Ji, in his *Bani Sukhmani Sahib*, said, '*Sagal Matant Keval Har Namm, Gobind Bhagat Ke Mann Bisram* (The theme of all Gurbani is the Name of the Creator. Whosoever connects to it becomes pure, and his mind comes to rest).'

There are three factors that can help identify Anahad Shabad or the cosmic sound.

1. We cannot hear it with our ears. In other words, we can hear it even if we shut our ears with cotton. In fact, we do not 'hear' it at all, we experience it—because it is not a sound, it is the being of our soul. We experience it with our Dhyan. To be more precise, we rest in our Dhyan or soul. It is an experience that transcends our body and mind, the material world or nature. The being or happening of our soul is beyond space and time. When we start experiencing it constantly, we transcend space and time.

2. It is present everywhere. There is no space without it. It is present in each and every particle of the universe. We may call it omnipresent.

3. It is beyond time. It is present at all times. Kabir called it 'Sahaj Samadhi'. He said,

Santo Sahaj Smadh Bhali, Jab te Daya Bhai Satgur ki, Surat Na Bhool Chali, Jahan Jahan Jae soi Prikarma, Jo Jo Kre So Pooja. Ghar Bhahar Sabh ek sam Bhase, Bhao mete sab dooja. Shabad Adhar se sune Niranter, Sagal Vasna Tiage, Jagat Sovat Uthath Baetath Gaheri Tari Lagae Aankh Nan Mundun Kaan Nan Rundun,

Kanyan Kashat Nan Dharun Oughre nain nij sahib daikhun, Sunder Roop Niharun. Kahen Kabir Ehe Uttam Rehni Pargat Kahe so Gai Sukh Dukh Pre Param Pad Darse Soi Sada Sukh Dai

Kabir says to holy people, experiencing your soul is bliss. When the Creator blessed me, I never forgot this experience and continued to rest in Dhyan for ever. Now wherever I go, I travel to him and whatever I do, I worship him. Now I am one with the universe and have realized that there is no other. I am listening to the Anhad Shabad without any gap, and all distractions in my mind have vanished. Whether awake, sleeping, standing, or sitting, I remain deeply connected. I no longer need to perform painful austerities, I see his beauty everywhere with my blessed eyes.

In the end, Kabir says, 'What I have explained is optimum living, which is beyond joy and sorrow. It is the world of Ananda, and it is forever.'

The Ninth Sikh Guru

The eighth Sikh Guru, Shri Harikrishan Ji, was only seven years old when he breathed his last. His last words were, 'Baba Bakala,' meaning that the next Guru is at Bakala, a place near Amritsar in Punjab. As a result, twenty-two different people started claiming to be the Guru, and the Sikh Sangat was in a fix as to whom they should accept.

Meanwhile, a businessman named Makhan Shah Labana

was traveling in his ship back to his hometown when a cyclone struck the ocean. Seeing no hope for survival, he prayed to the seat of Guru Nanak and pledged to offer five hundred gold Mohars (coins) to the present Guru if he returned home safe.

The cyclone drifted away, and he reached his home safely. Loyal to his pledge, he went to Bakala to present his offering to the Guru. But upon reaching Bakala, to his shock, there were twenty-two of them in line! He quickly thought of a plan and offered five gold Mohars to each of them. Once all of them had been paid off, he asked if anyone was left. He was told that a person named Tega was sitting in an underground room. As Makhan Shah was unsatisfied with his offering, he went to the underground room and offered the standard five gold Mohars. Tega responded, 'You pledged five hundred, and now you are offering five?'

Makhan Shah was stunned. He ran out, excited, and began shouting from the rooftops, '*Guru Ladho Re, Guru Ladho Re* (the Guru has been found, the Guru has been found)!'

Tega had been listening to the sound of Anhad Shabad— experiencing his soul—sitting in the room underground for the last twenty years.

After he was declared the ninth Sikh Guru, he became Shri Guru Teg Bahadur Sahib, who stood against a powerful king, Aurangzeb, for the cause of religious freedom for everyone. He sacrificed his life and became a great martyr.

A long time back, a New Yorker came to know about

a Buddha meditation centre in the city of Rangoon (now Yangon), the capital of Burma (now Myanmar). He planned to attend the three-week meditation course and boarded a plane to Rangoon. He fantasized about a place near a canal surrounded by trees, in the middle of a valley, peaceful and beautiful. He hoped to rest for three weeks, away from the mad crowds of New York. But when his taxi stood in front of the meditation centre, he was furious. He could not believe what he was seeing. It was in the middle of a fish market in a narrow bazaar. There were all kinds of noises all around. People were shouting at the top of their voices, stray dogs were fighting over leftover fish, and a murder of crows were cawing shrilly. Pigs were grunting in their own strange way. There was an all-pervasive stink. He could not stand the scene, and thought of going back in the same taxi. But to his dismay, there were no flights for the next three days. He did not have any alternative but to stay there for three days.

He went into the centre and asked the Guru, 'Why is this centre in such a dirty place?' The Guru told him that it was too early to answer his question. He would answer after a week. Now the New Yorker began looking around and saw some Bodhi Monks meditating in their own ways. One was sitting under a tree and meditating; another was walking while meditating; yet another was lying on the grass, completely absorbed; and one was standing against a wall, equally absorbed. Some were carrying out routine chores. He realized that every monk was peaceful; their faces were graceful and bright, and they did not seem to be disturbed by the noises and the environment. He began realizing that he was missing something important.

The next morning, he attended the meditation class and his lessons began. After three days, he found that the noises and the atmosphere were a little less disturbing and he felt like extending his stay for at least one more week. After a week, he was so absorbed that he did not go to the Guru for the answer—he simply extended his stay to three weeks, till the completion of the course. He began enjoying meditation and forgot all about the noises and the environment. Once the course was complete, he wanted to extend his stay further, but could not. He went to see the Guru before departing and said, 'My question was wrong.' The Guru smiled and told him, 'That is why this meditation centre is here. You now understand very well what peace and stability it has brought to you. Now you may go to any disturbed place in the world, but you will remain peaceful and stable.'

Meditation is simply resting in the soul or the true nature, which is divine. While resting in your true nature, you transcend cosmic duality and settle in peace. You remain peaceful under even the most difficult circumstances. You become the Blessed One.

Karma and Salvation

Our mind does not know anything beyond the material world, because it is subtle material itself. All that we do in this material world using our ten bodily senses gets accumulated in our memory as impressions. These past impressions are called karmas. They can be a mixture of good and bad impressions. They decide our behaviour, likes, dislikes, desires, addictions, habits, actions and reactions. A man is a product of these past impressions. When living in the physical world, he needs to have good impressions in his memory. That is why the development of the human mind is given so much importance.

We educate our children and develop their habits, behaviour and skills. We train them in good cultures to make them good human beings. By doing this, we feed good data into their memory, which they reproduce when they grow up. But whatever we might do to develop their minds, they are still products of the mind and continue to operate through the mind. To make them real human beings, we must connect them to their souls. When they are connected to their souls, they go beyond the mind and karmas. Only then can they reach their full potential.

Buddhists believe that our lives unfold according to the natural law of cause and effect, which they call the Law of Karma. It means that our present circumstances are a result of our past actions and thoughts. Even though life flows as naturally and inevitably as a river or as the changing of seasons, our future is always shaped by how we choose to act in the present. The more we can see through our greed, anger and ignorance, the more satisfying will our future circumstances be.

Human beings are prisoners of their past impressions, lying in their memory. Most of the time, they are driven by their memory. They continue to be slaves of their minds and lead stale lives. A life lived through the mind is a repetition of some old life, over and over. You keep repeating the same actions, the same dialogues and the same addictions. You continue living in the past and the future. Most people lead these stale lives for years and years and die without ever knowing a fresh one.

When you get connected to your soul, you transcend your mind and karmas. Now you are no more a slave of your mind—you are its master; your mind behaves the way you want it to, as you have won your self-control back by connecting to yourself. Now you stop hopping between the past and the future and start living in the present. You are born to live in the present. In the present there are no karmas, no past impressions, no mind, no ego, and no negative energies. You are all positive energy. Life is fresh and always new. While living in the present, all of your senses are free. Whatever you do with your free senses becomes worship or Yog, as there is no leakage of Dhyan. You are doing everything with 100 per cent Dhyan. The Gita says that whatever you do with 100 per cent Dhyan becomes Yog. This is the optimum life you are born to live.

When a human is disconnected from the soul

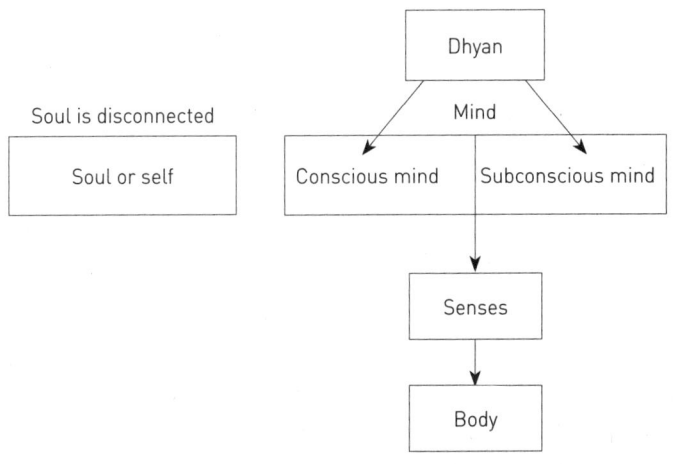

In this case, Dhyan is flowing through the conscious and the subconscious minds. All karmas lying in the subconscious mind are growing, flowering and bearing fruit, and humans will have to reap it.

In the present, your Dhyan remains connected to the soul and does not flow into the subconscious mind—as Dhyan is the power upon which all karmas grow, flower and bear fruits that you reap. When Dhyan stops flowing into the subconscious mind, all the fruits of karmas dry out like a crop dying out for lack of water. Then you become free from karmas—as in the present, with your all senses

free, you do everything with 100 per cent Dhyan—so no
further karmas are formed and you remain free of karmas
forever.

When a human being is connected to the soul

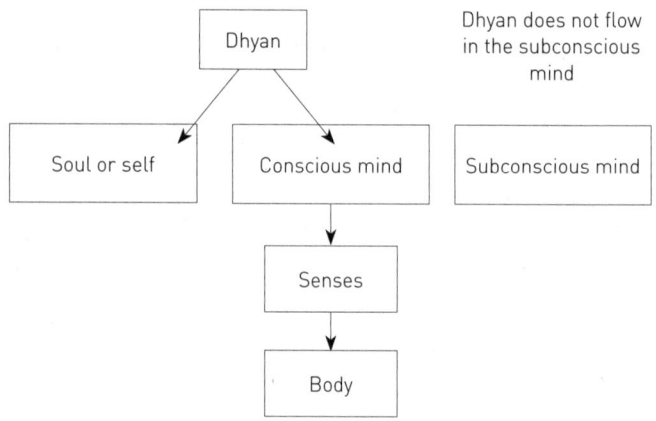

Here, the human is awakened and Dhyan rests in the
soul and flows through the conscious mind only. Dhyan
does not flow in the subconscious mind. So the crop of
all your karmas dries out without Dhyan power, just as a
green crop dries out without water

About the mind, Guru Nanak said,

Andhla neech Jat Pardesi
Khin Aave til jave,
Tan ki sangat nanak rahenda
Phir kaun moorha pave.

(The human mind is blind, cheap and a stranger. It comes
for a moment and then runs away. If our soul has the mind

for company, how can it rest in the divine?)

Nothing you do in this physical world can satisfy you. You keep longing for more, unaware that even that will not satisfy you. In fact, it is not a longing for more—it is a longing to become one with the universe. When you get settled in yourself, you become one with the universe. Then whatever little you are doing is more than enough, and you become fully satisfied.

Ashtavakra said, 'Think of your tendencies and distractions as poison' and discard them, and think of forgiveness, compassion, peace, innocence and contentment as Amrit (nectar) and embrace them. Leave your body and mind, and rest in consciousness (Dhyan).'

The whole cosmic order is unconditional manifestation. Everything, except human beings, is reconciled to living unconditional manifestation. A seed ruptures and a plant takes birth, it grows, flowers and bears fruits. Further, fruits carry seeds inside. Plants grow old and die. Similarly, for human beings, a child takes birth, grows into an adult, reproduces, grows old and dies. This is the unconditional cycle of manifestation, which cannot be disrupted. But only human beings do not believe in this cosmic cycle. They believe in 'I am,' and this 'I am' is the factory of all our karmas, ego, negative energies and suffering.

Ashtavakra said, 'Your wrong perception of "I am" has given birth to karmas. In fact, there is no "I am". You are not a body and mind, you are a soul. The entire universe has only one soul, so you are one with the universe.'

Your Dhyan has the power of concentration, so whereever

you concentrate it, so you become. You concentrated it on
'I am' so you became 'I am', and for all karmas committed
by the body and the mind, you became responsible. You
owned all of these karmas due to incorrect perception. Said
Ashtavakra, 'Correct your perception and realize that that
you are not body and mind, that you are a soul and a non-
Doer, so these karmas do not belong to you and you are
not responsible for them. You will become free of your
karmas. You are already free—simply drop your incorrect
perception.'

Shri Ramakrishan said,

'All is divine, whether in form or without form. You
are divine too. Perceive everybody to be as divine as
yourself, then there are no karmas and no suffering—
you live in peace in Ananda.'

Optimum Living

We run after whatever our mind desires, thinking that we can satisfy it and settle in happiness one day. But the more we do so, the more it remains unsatisfied. This is the basic nature of our mind. It is like trying to extinguish a fire by pouring oil on it.

In order to satisfy our mind, we work hard. We don't notice an obvious fact—we have been working hard since a very young age, but has the mind ever been satisfied? Our mind is the source of all our tendencies, all our distractions, all negative energy, and all leakage of the superpower of Dhyan. It is dissipating our superpower and making us miserable.

Running after the mind's desires has nothing to do with real happiness. Happiness comes from settling in our basic nature—resting in our soul. Only when we rest in peace inside is our mind most satisfied and happy. We then become truly powerful and wise, and can do everything effortlessly. The things that we were running after now run after us. Things that were out of reach are easily accessible now.

Upon reaching this stage, we need not work hard any longer. We were working hard as we were weak, due to the leakage of the superpower of Dhyan. The more our superpower leaks, the weaker we grow and the harder we have to work to do a certain thing, which would have been effortless had we been at peace within.

Imagine two wrestlers wrestling in a field. If one is injured and bleeding badly, he will have to put in more effort to win than the one who is relatively uninjured and not bleeding.

So to live in peace and happiness, we need to settle down in our basic nature.

The Creator has given us the beautiful power of imagination in order to create new things to make this world worth living in, but we use this power to think of negative things, resulting in negative events, which then scare us. We call this fear 'fear of the unknown'. Similarly, we imagine suspicion, hatred, greed, jealousy, guilt and all other negative energies. If we witness our negative energies effectively, we can use them to our benefit and turn them into positive energies. We can use our anger to effectively witness our negative energy. We can nurture a greed to serve society. We can develop hate for stale living. We can become jealous of a man who lives in peace and harmony, and try to become like him.

Upon analysis, we will find that the fear of the unknown and suspicion are the principal negative energies that are crippling our lives.

What is fear of the unknown?

We become anxious about potential negative situations, even if we know that they may not come to pass. Most of these fears come from overpossessiveness or attachment. We do not want to lose what we are attached to. We keep on imagining negative things about them and thus being afraid. These fears creep into our subconscious mind and become routine behaviours.

Similarly, suspicion is also a negative energy. We suspect that a person may be vengeful and harbor a grudge against us, when in reality he or she may not be bothered at all. Imagining negative things about someone changes our behaviour towards the person and results in dire consequences.

Kabir said, 'What you imagine about others is what is inside you.'

Similarly, all other negative energies are imaginary—that is why they are deficiencies of Dhyan. If you witness your negative energies effectively, they will vanish and you will feel free and pleasant.

A young boy asked his grandfather, 'When I switch off the light in my room at night, I become afraid. What should I do?'

The grandfather asked the boy, 'What are you afraid of?' The boy thought for a while and replied, 'That there might be something dangerous inside my room.'

The grandfather asked, 'Why are you imagining false things? First you conjure up a false thing in your imagination, then you become afraid of it. Then why imagine it at all?'

The boy understood his folly and laughed. After this,

he was never afraid.

This is how we imagine false things in our lives and become afraid of them.

Human sorrows can be compared to a dark room. Darkness is merely a deficiency of light, just as sorrows are merely a deficiency of Dhyan. When you enter a dark room you become suspicious and then afraid, just as when you are in sorrow. If you want to expel the darkness, bring a light into the room. The darkness will leave automatically. Everything will become clear, and there will no longer be any suspicion or fear. Similarly, to expel sorrow, bring Dhyan into your life. Suspicion and fear will also vanish. So an abundance of Dhyan, which you receive after connecting to your soul or resting in yourself or through meditation, is the only solution to all your sorrows.

In Zen practice, we try to experience life without the interference of the opinions and ideas we have accumulated. And then, because all our senses are free to focus without distractions, we become aware of all kind of things we otherwise would not have noticed. We can even sense that the life in a tree is not so different from our own. At that point we reach a level of perception that the Zen Masters call 'Intimacy', or 'no separation'. Zen teaches that when we are most aware, there is no feeling of separation between subject and object. We experience the space inside and outside of ourselves as continuous. Now, because every moment is new, we become new, because we are not separate from the moments. Zen masters say that we should experience our lives as if for the first time without any of our old fears and prejudices. If we can forget the instinct to protect our separate selves and let life in completely, we can have a really good time.

Zen teaches single-mindedness, whole-heartedness, intimacy, direct-perception, non-aggression and spontaneity—a total transformation of our whole being and behaviour, affecting all aspects of our life.

Swami Vivekananda delivered a soul-stirring discourse on the non-dualistic philosophy of Advaita in America. He said:

> All is Atman; there is neither existence nor nonexistence. Shake off all ideas of relativity. Shake off all superstitions. Let caste, birth, the Devas and all else vanish.
>
> Why talk of being and becoming? Give up talking of dualism and even Advaita. When were you two, that you talk of two or one?
>
> The universe is the Holy one—and he alone. Talk not of yoga to make you pure, you are pure by your very nature. None can teach you.

He surprised the whole world with the ancient wisdom of oneness.

Let us consider the body. If we are sick, our Dhyan will continue to leak till we recover. So it is necessary to be healthy. Taking care of our health is very important. We must take balanced food in proper instalments and with proper timing. Then we must exercise to maintain the shape and flexibility of our bodies. We must take care of our cleanliness and clothing. We must ensure that our health is not an issue. When we are healthy, the body ceases to be a reason for the leakage of Dhyan.

Then let us consider our mind. Our mind is full of impurities. It is the main cause of the leakage of our Dhyan. We can take care of our mind by adding more positive data to its memory, doing selfless service, keeping good company, detaching from addictions, and reading about the lives of great people. We must imprint in our memory that we are not Doers. Doership is the main cause of negative energy and Dhyan leakage. We should witness our thoughts so that negative thoughts are filtered out and do not enter our memory. Our mind is restless because of impurities. If it is purified, it comes to rest and we are able to connect to our soul.

Now, let us consider our soul. We should become connected to our soul and experience it. When we experience it—which we call meditation—then an abundance of Dhyan energy flows through us and we experience Ananda. Our Dhyan level increases.

With more experience, we start living in an abundance of Dhyan and our negative energies become neutralized, as they are simply a deficiency of Dhyan. We become all positive energy, and minor Dhyan leakage no longer affects our peace and stability. Now we can live in true freedom, with a purified mind and constantly connected to our soul. With the blessings of the divine, this is truly optimum living.

The mind is a material. The mind and all its activities are the source of gravity, which keeps pulling you down to the material world. Dhyan is a positive energy. When connected to Dhyan, you will be in high spirits and free from the material world. When you start being in Dhyan all the time, you become free from the gravity of the material world and complete freedom prevails unto you.

Shri Guru Ram Das Ji said:

Lechha Purak Sarab Sukh data Har,
Ja Kae Vas Hae Kaam Dhaena.
So Aesa Har Dhyiyae Mare Jeearhae,
Tan Sarab Sukh Paveh Mare Manna,
Jap Man Sat Naam Sada Sat Naam,
Halat Palat Mukh Ujjal Hoi Hae,
Nitt Dhyiyae Har Purkh Niranjana.
Jaeh Har Simiran Bhaiya Taeh Upadh
Gat Keeni, Vadbhaghi Har Japna.
Jan Nanak Kauo Gur Eah Mat
Deeni, Jap Har Bhavjal Tarna.

(Fulfiler of desires, giver of pleasure and happiness and controller of all material wealth is your almighty soul. Satguru says to the human mind that if you want to enjoy this physical world, then experience your powerful soul. He further says that if you experience it constantly, you will be blessed in both worlds. He says that where the soul is being experienced, there is a flood of positive energy, which delivers good fortune. In the end, he says that only the blessed ones act on his advice to experience their souls, and they transcend this physical world after fully enjoying it.)

PART-2

FREE YOUR DHYAN TO LIVE IN PEACE
AND ANANDA FOREVER

Some Thoughts

Our restlessness in the material world is due to our cravings. We are not satisfied with what we have. When we deeply introspect and find that what we have is more than enough, our craving disappears and we become free and peaceful.

When we do something selfless for others we feel happy. Because in reality, there is no 'other'. This selfless act unites us with the universe and we feel oneness. It is our true nature.

We are living our life in glimpses. When something unites us with our self, we feel joy, and when something separates us from the self, we feel sorrow. When we are honoured we feel joy, when we are abused we feel sorrow. When we remain united with ourself all the time, we go beyond joy and sorrow and transcend this material world of glimpses and settle in peace and Ananda.

Introduction

The human body and mind and their activities are solid and subtle materials. They belong to the Earth. These materials have gravity, which is always pulling people down to the material world. But a human being's Dhyan is spirit. It belongs to the sky. It frees him or her from the material gravity.

If his/her Dhyan level is high enough and he is perpetually connected to his Dhyan (self), as he was at the time of his birth, then he becomes free from the gravity of the material world and settles in peace and Ananda forever.

You Are the Whole Universe

The true nature of a human is Ananda, Sehaj, rest or nothing. When he is in his true nature, he is limitless or all-powerful. When he becomes something else, he becomes limited, with limited powers and limited joy. This leads to blockages and limited thinking, which further leads to hopping between the past and the future. When he is in his true nature, he lives in the present with unlimited thinking, which means that he lives in the past, present and future at the same time.

The entire universe is a soul. It is a single organism. It is charged with the positive energy which is called Soul or Dhyan. Everything in the universe belongs to this soul. You also belong to this soul. Your soul and the soul of the whole universe is the same.

As the whole universe is a soul, you are walking in the soul, you are talking in the soul, sleeping in the soul, working in the soul and doing everything in the same soul. In other words, your soul is the whole universe itself. Which means you are the whole universe, or you may say that this whole universe is your extension. You are not separate—

you are part and parcel of this universe. This universe is a single, dynamic, interdependent whole.

Take the example of the electric train. Two grooved electric conductors are laid overhead from one corner to another corner of the country, spanning thousands of kilometres. These conductors are charged with a high voltage electric current. These are stationary—they do not move and are always at rest. Every train makes overhead contact with these conductors and moves on. Thousands of trains are running every day powered by the electricity through these charged conductors, but these conductors do not move at all—they remain at rest.

Grooved conductors charged
with high-voltage electric
current at rest

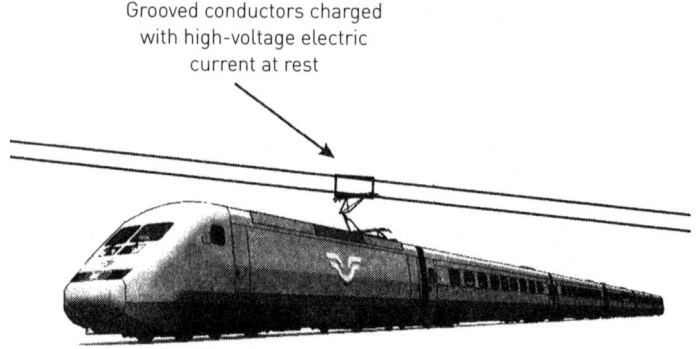

Train moves but electric conductors remain always at rest

Similarly, everything in this universe is moving or working because of the positive energy of the soul and this soul remains ever stationary or at rest. So our soul or the soul of the universe remains always at rest—that is why when we get connected to our soul we come to rest. Conversely, when we come to rest from within, we get connected to our soul.

Now it is clear that we are the whole universe, as our soul and the soul of the universe is the same. Then who is the 'other'? There is no 'other'. So the 'other' is our false perception. Then whatsoever we do for the so-called 'other' we are, in fact, doing for ourselves.

If we do good for the 'other', we do good for ourselves and if we do bad for the 'other', we do bad for ourselves. If we have good intentions for 'others' we have good intentions for ourselves. If we have bad intentions for 'others' we have bad intentions for ourselves. What does this mean? This means that what we want for ourselves, we should do for 'others'.

When we want to scare the other or take revenge on them, we end up scaring or hurting ourselves. Only when we abandon these desires can we settle in peace and become powerful enough to be fearless.

Similarly, we get hatred when we spread hatred. We get love when we spread love. We get in abundance what we contribute to this holy universe.

The Bible says, 'Love thy neighbour.' Here, 'neighbour' denotes everybody connected to you. If everybody loves his neighbour, then there will be peace in the world.

The Universe According to Science

All materials are made up of over a hundred elements. These elements are made of a few particles and the particles are made of energy, and energy is made of rays of different wavelengths and frequencies.

Electromagnetism and gravity make up three dimensions of space—length, width, and height. The fourth dimension is time—the order of events. Interaction between electro magnetism and gravity makes matter energy, which falls under the constraints of space and time.

Matter and energy are the same thing.

Space and consciousness are the same thing.

Space and time are the same thing.

As space and consciousness are without borders, everything falls within them. They give birth to everything, sustain things throughout their lives and absorb them back after their lives. This means people have come from space and consciousness, and have to go back to the same after life. This consciousness is the human soul, or Dhyan. When a a human gets connected to his/her soul, he or she transcends space and time and becomes limitless.

Inner Peace

In order to live our optimum life, we need to have inner peace. When we are peaceful inside, we live a life of Ananda.

The moment we know that we are one with the whole universe and everyone is our extension and we are all interdependent on each other, we settle in oneness with the universe. When we further know that whatsoever we do for others we are doing for ourselves, we settle in harmony with the universe. This oneness and living in harmony gives us inner peace. This inner peace is the most valuable possession in this world.

How Do We live?

We live away from the truth. We do not know the truth and take decisions on the basis of our past impressions or hearsay, further embellishing it in our imaginations. This cannot take us to the truth, because data of our past impressions is stale data. It belongs to the past, whereas a person or a situation changes every moment. To know the truth, we have to be at rest peaceful and quiet from within. At this stage, we are closer to the truth because the mind does not distract us. Now we can take the right decisions, which will lead us to better results.

Universal Interdependence

Nothing is independent in this universe. Everybody and everything is interdependent on each other. The more we move towards our original nature, the more we come to know that we are all united with this universe and dependent on it.

Let us take the example of a human being. Where was he when his parents had not yet been born? At some point, his parents were born, they matured, and they mated according to the natural laws of reproduction. The young mother conceived and the child took birth at the right time. He took his first breath and began growing into an adult. Once again, he found an adult partner, and had a child of their own. The cycle of reproduction continued.

Now, the parents of this young couple grow old and die, going back to where they came from. They came to this world from Dhyan and went back, after death, to Dhyan. It is the Dhyan energy that gave them birth, sustained them throughout their lives, and after death, absorbed them back into it.

From this cycle of our life, we come to know that we

have never been independent, not even for a moment. We are ever-dependent on the universe.

It is Dhyan that empowers a seed to rupture and sprout a seedling. It is Dhyan that gives it leaves and branches and stems to turn it into a beautiful plant. It is Dhyan that empowers it to flower and bear fruits. Fruits again have seeds, which grow into more such plants. When you observe deeply, you find evidence everywhere that Dhyan is running the whole universe. Without Dhyan this whole universe is a lump of dust.

Now the plant grows old and dies. It goes back to where it came from. This is the cycle of every living, and every non-living, thing. There is not a single particle of dust that has not been recycled endlessly.

Nature has blessed us with all types of foods, fruits, flowers, and medicinal plants. All types of weather, mountains, forests and rivers. If we take the example of a fruit and think about how it has grown, we will see the seed that was sown, but also the fertile soil with all its nutrients, and water, sun, air, and space, along with human efforts—all of which contributed to its birth and growth. The soil in which the seed was sown has been recycled countless times. We do not know how many of our ancestors, alongside animals and plants, have been buried after death in this soil and added to its fertility. The fruits we are eating contain entire histories we do not know about. Once we realize this, what happens to our self-dependence? As is evident, we are totally interdependent.

We are sharing air with all living beings—people,

animals, birds, insects, plants, etc. We are sharing water, vegetation, sunlight, moonlight, space and everything else with the entire universe.

Even inside our minds, we are not alone. We are a crowd. When we come to know that we are not independent— that we are interdependent—our egos get dissolved and with it the cosmic duality between subject and object gets dissolved. We experience our true nature, which is oneness with the universe.

Every human in the universe functions like a micro-radio station. We emit and receive energy according to our Dhyan level. If the Dhyan level is very low due to leakage owing to the presence of negative energy, our frequency of emission will be low and we will receive, in return, energy of the same frequency—which means that a person emitting negative energy will receive more negative energy from the universe in return. It will result in more leakage of Dhyan.

This means sorrows invite more sorrows.

A person with a high level of Dhyan will emit energy at a high frequency and receive energy of the same frequency. This means he emits positive energy and receives more positive energy from the universe. Which further means that joy invites more joy.

When a person is perpetually connected to Dhyan, his Dhyan level becomes very high. He becomes the source of positive energy and emits positive energy at a very high frequency. An abundance of positive energy flows through him on this planet, which helps in neutralizing negative energy. Human words cannot express the contribution of such a person to mankind.

When we see terrorism, oppression and cruelty all around us, it shows us that the Dhyan level of the earth has fallen very low. This can be improved by raising the Dhyan level of a large number of people. This will neutralize the effect of negative energy and peace will return.

Human Identity

Our planet, Earth, is like a small particle in the enormous cosmic order. In this small particle live seven billion people, countless animals, birds, plants, rivers, mountains, oceans and deserts. From this we can make out the identity of a human being, which he denotes through the words 'I am.'

This 'I am' is not his true identity, it is a fake identity. His true identity is his soul, or Dhyan, or consciousness, which is the whole universe itself. So a single human is the whole universe, which he realizes as soon as he drops his fake identity. Then he lives in unconditional manifestation, which is his true nature.

As soon as he drops his fake identity of 'I am' he transcends his body and mind and comes out of a material world of joy, sorrow and bondage and enters his true nature, 'Ananda.'

In his true nature, there is no birth and death. As the soul is a non-Doer, eternal, permanent, constant, self-shining, self-knowing and all-powerful, a human resting in his true nature is free from karma, because karmas belong to the body and the mind—or nature, which is the Doer.

When we recognize this reality and identify ourselves and separate our body and mind from the self, we start witnessing everything and we run out of karmas. Our soul is the observer or witness of everything in this universe. When we become witnesses, we come out of Doership. We come to rest in our true nature of peace and Ananda.

The Uniqueness of the Human Body
(Where the Devil and God Live Together)

People live in two worlds: the material world and the Dhyan world. These worlds exist opposite each other.

The material world is ever-changing, temporary, dual, impure, restless and full of negative energy.

The Dhyan world is constant, eternal, non-dual, pure, peaceful and full of positive energy.

Both of these worlds are reflected in the human body. This body is so unique that a person is capable of moving in both of these worlds.

Two Worlds of Humanity

Material World: Body and Mind	Dhyan World: Soul or Dhyan
Human body: Solid material Human mind and its activities: Subtle material All these materials can be seen or witnessed.	Dhyan or consciousness or awareness. It cannot be witnessed as it is a witness itself. Our soul is a witness

Matter (Decaying)	Spirit (Eternal)

People live in both of these worlds, as their bodies and minds are part of nature, which is run by soul or Dhyan.

The human body has seven energy centres. These provide seven different types of strengths or powers to people, in order for them to live in these worlds. The centres are—root, sex, navel, heart, throat, the third eye and the crown chakra.

The heart energy centre, which is called the 'Anahat Chakra', lies at the centre of all of these seven energy centres. It is the centre where we feel love and compassion, and open our hearts to the non-judgmental, detached universal love. The lower three energy centres—root, sex and navel—represent the material world and the upper three energy centres—throat, third eye and crown chakra—represent the Dhyan world.

When the Dhyan of a person moves to the lower three centres, he lives in the material world of joy, sorrow and bondage, as he is not connected with his soul—he is controlled by his mind. Due to lack of self-control, he develops Doership, which gives birth to a brutal ego and reels in the negative energy that causes further leakage of his Dhyan energy and makes his life miserable.

The further down from the heart centre his Dhyan energy progresses, the more like a devil or an animal he becomes, until the transformation is complete at the root centre.

1) Root Chakra—Located at the base of the spine. Element: earth. This enables physical stability.

The Human Body's Seven Energy Centres (Chakras)

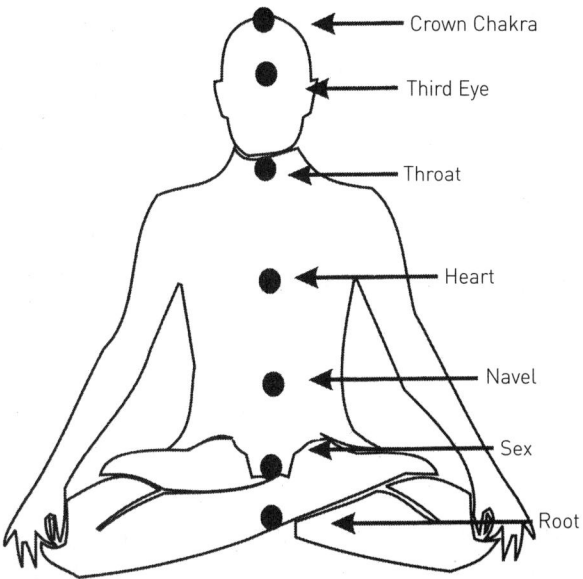

The heart energy centre is the centre of all the seven centres. The lower three energy centres—root, sex and navel—represent the material world and the upper three energy centres—throat, third eye and crown chakra—represent the Dhyan world.

2) Sex Chakra—Located in the genital region. Element: water. This enables effortless procreation.

3) Navel Chakra—Located at the navel. Element: fire. Ignites physical energy for sound health and physical power.

4) Heart Chakra—Located at the heart. Element: air. The centre of love, compassion and detached universal love.

5) Throat Chakra—Located in the throat. Element: space. Helps to fearlessly express our truth and hear the sound of the universe.

6) Third Eye Chakra—Located at the meeting point of the eyebrows. Concentrates Dhyan energy, imagination and intuition.

7) Crown Chakra—Located at the crown of the head. Connects with cosmic power or the universal soul.

When the Dhyan of a person moves to the upper three energy centres, he begins to move beyond the material world. As he moves up, his Dhyan level increases, with the result that his negative energy from the material world starts decreasing and he starts feeling peaceful and happy. The more he moves towards the crown chakra, the more peaceful and powerful he becomes. When he reaches the crown chakra, he gets connected to his soul or cosmic power and an abundance of Dhyan energy flows through his body, raising his Dhyan level to Godliness. He starts living a life of Ananda. At this stage, the mind becomes obedient, finally assuming its real place in the human body.

The human mind is conscious; thus human beings have the ability to free themselves from the material world. If a person has knowledge of both the worlds, he can connect himself to his soul and earnestly practise raising his Dhyan level through meditation to finally transcend the material world.

The main problem of human beings is that these two worlds are of contradictory natures, which gives rise to the contradictions of life.

In the material world, nothing can be achieved without effort. But the Dhyan world is the exact opposite—it is a world of rest or 'sehaj', and you need to abandon effort to enter it. Effort is an obstacle in the Dhyan world.

So people have to make an effort to come out of the material world, and then abandon that effort to enter the Dhyan world.

According to Ashtavakra, 'The human heart becomes trapped in complexity, but the solution to every problem lies here. If we can untangle this knot of complexity, every human problem can be solved and we can free ourselves from the material world.'

The fifth Sikh Guru, Shri Guru Arjun Dev Ji, in his *Banni Sukhmani Sahib*, said, *'Barham Maen Jan, Jan maen Parbraham. Aekah Aap Nahin Kichhu Bharam* (People exist in the universe and in them exist the Creator of the universe. The Creator exists in everything, without any doubt).'

Raja Janak once told his guru Ashtavakra, 'When I experienced my own Creator in this body, with your blessings, I got so overwhelmed that I wanted to touch my own feet, because I could experience my own Creator— the Creator of the whole universe—while living in this body. So this body has become dearer to me.'

Shri Guru Ram Das Ji has the following Bani:

Wiche Dharti Wiche Panni Wich Kaast Agan Dhareejae, Bakri Singh Eakton Thain Rakhae, Mann Har jap Bharam Bhao Duur Keejae.

(It is surprising how the Creator has managed to keep
earth, water and fire together in the human body. He
has also managed to keep the goat and the lion in the
same place. In order to dispel your suspicion and fear,
you must experience your soul.)

He essentially explains that the human body contains earth,
water and fire, which represent the root, sex and navel
energy centres respectively. He further explains that the
heart is the one place where the goat and the lion may
be kept together. The goat represents human fear and the
lion fearlessness; they also represent the devil and God,
respectively. Only the Creator is capable of allowing this
miracle to happen.

We become increasingly afraid when our Dhyan moves
down from the heart, with our fear becoming most dreadful
at the root. Likewise, when it moves up, our fear slowly
dissipates, until we become totally fearless at the crown.

Shri Guru Amardas Ji says:

*Har Mandir Eah Sarir Hae. Gian Ratan Pargat Hoe
Manmukh Mool Na Jan Eee Manas Har Mandir Na
Hoe.*

(This human body is a temple to the Creator of the
universe, which provides pearls of knowledge that
allow us to unite with him. The ignorant knows not
that his ego is not the temple.)

We Are Prisoners of Our Minds

Disconnection from our soul has left us at the mercy of our minds. The mind is like a mechanical instrument. Whatever we do with the ten senses of our body is collected in our memory or subconscious mind in the form of good and bad impressions. These past impressions drive us 80 per cent of the time. Our bodily senses are preoccupied with these past impressions. They needlessly keep recalling the good and bad events of the past and thus keep living in the dream world of joy and sorrow and bondage.

We may glimpse the most beautiful things, but we ignore them because our senses are busy in recalling past impressions. This is how we keep losing the chances of a fresh life and keep living a stale one.

We need to keep all our senses free in order to live a fresh life. Then we shall be able to enjoy each and every moment as it comes to us in its original form. We shall no longer be prisoners of the mind, and will have freed ourselves from addiction to past impressions.

This is possible only if we go beyond our mind by

connecting ourselves with our soul, and are able to exercise our self-control.

Our mind is a very important instrument. We cannot live in the material world without it. Our mind receives consciousness or Dhyan from superconsciousness and delivers it to our sense organs in order for us to lead our lives. But in the absence of our connection with the soul, it becomes a source of distraction.

The mind, in its original form, is as pure as the soul, but due to impurities it becomes a source of distraction. The main impurity is 'I am'. This incorrect perception of 'I am' or ego corrupts our mind. All impressions collected in the memory through 'I am' are addictive to the mind. Since the mind is material itself, it cannot properly differentiate between good and bad and exercise its self-control until supported by the soul or Dhyan.

The mind is the instrument that receives consciousness from superconsciousness. Its capacity to receive this depends on the purity of the mind at the time of reception. When the mind is impure, it receives a lower quantity of consciousness than when it is pure. When the mind is purified, it comes to rest and becomes enlightened. It gets connected to the soul and starts receiving a large quantity of consciousness, which takes us to an abundance of Dhyan. We are born to live in an abundance of Dhyan. When we live in an abundance of Dhyan, we are no longer prisoners of the mind. We live a fresh and new life every moment. That is living in the present.

In order to have a healthy mind, we must take care of

it. We must feed purified and good data to the memory. We can purify data by witnessing our thoughts and actions. We need to keep our minds away from addictions or stale living. We must develop our minds for healthy practices, healthy thoughts and healthy relations.

All our religious books are addressed to the human mind, in order to develop it and make this world a peaceful and healthy place to live in. We need to feed these experiences of great people to our minds to make them healthy and restful.

Your mind continues dragging you to past impressions even after you get connected to your soul, but as soon as you witness this, you come out immediately. When you are not connected, it keeps dragging you back for hours upon hours and you lose your mighty Dhyan Power.

We suffer in life because our soul is badly trapped in the material world. In order to be peaceful, we are to free our soul from it. Our body is solid material and our mind is subtle material. Everything produced by our body and mind is material. Our feelings, likes and dislikes, desires, thoughts, imagination, intentions, love, hatred, dreams, perceptions, habits, addictions and all our past impressions in our subconscious minds are materials. These materials have gravity, which keeps pulling us down to the material world. It is the reason behind our negative energies and suffering.

Our Dhyan iş spirit, which belongs to the sky. Thus it pulls us out from the gravity of the material world. The greater our Dhyan level, the more we are pulled out. When our Dhyan level grows very high, we are completely pulled out of the gravity of the material world. This means we have freed our self (our soul) while still alive. So in order to be in peace and Ananda, or in the present, we must increase our Dhyan level.

The world has seen people invading other countries and starting world wars because of their minds' greed. It has seen terrorism; it has seen partition of nations and consequent brutality for the same reason. The world has also seen gurus and prophets who spread peace and liberated mankind from their miseries and showed them the path to peace, to living in oneness and Ananda. The difference between these two types of people is the 'connection with the soul'. The former kind are disconnected, and the latter are connected to their souls.

As smoke clouds the air and obstructs our visibility of objects, similarly, negative energy clouds the soul and obstructs its experience. When the smoke is cleared, the air becomes clean and all objects are clearly visible; similarly, when the subconscious mind is purified, experiencing the soul becomes easy. Then you can clearly see the traits of the mind.

You are trapped in the subconscious mind due to lower alertness, when your Dhyan level is low. When your Dhyan level is high, you are most alert, and you no longer move in the subconscious mind. Even if you are trapped for a moment now and then, you come out by witnessing it immediately, as your witness is very powerful because of the high Dhyan level.

That is why experiencing the soul is also called

awakening. When you perpetually experience your soul you no longer get trapped in the subconscious mind. Your Dhyan level rises and you gain self-control. Your witnessing power becomes effective enough to witness the traits and thoughts of the mind. The mind comes under self-control and starts obeying nature's call or natural instincts. So your health in regained, your addictions are finished and excessive attachment and hooks are removed. You become a free person full of peace and stability.

There is nothing wrong with the human or material world—the only 'wrong' is entanglement of Dhyan in the material world or the human mind. When a person becomes a witness and starts witnessing this material world or his mind, he establishes his self separately from the non-self, and gains self-control.

The Guru says,

1. *Mann mare sukh sehaj sati*
   Jap Naon, Aath Pahar
   Prabh Dhiae toon Gunh
   Gobind nit Gaon

   (My mind experiences your soul being at rest and peace. Experience it all twenty four hours, and praise your Creator every day.)

2. *Mann toon Jout Sarup haen,*
   Apna mool Pachhan,
   Mann har ji Tare nal hae
   Gurmatti Rang Manh.

   (Mind, you are a divine light; recognize your source. Your Creator is always with you—enjoy your life according to the Guru's advice.)

3. *Mann Re Kaun Kumatt taen*
   Lini, Par Dara Nindia ras
   Rachio, Ram Bhagat Naeh Kini

   (Mind, such a wrong path you are following. Women and the criticism of others give you pleasure, but you do not worship your Creator.)

4. *Mare Mann Har Siun Lagi*
   Preet, Sadh Sang Har Har
   Japat, Nirmal Sachi Reet.

(My mind got connected to the soul and started experiencing it along with the holy men, accessing pure and true wisdom.)

Formation of Negative Energy or Deficiency of Dhyan

Normally, people are under the control of their subconscious minds, not their souls. This makes them see only what they want to see and hear only what they wish to hear. For example, a young, lustful man may misconstrue a piece of red cloth caught on a bush and flapping in the air as a beautiful dancing woman, from a distance. His fantasies will be further fed by his past impressions or desires. This will make him leak his mighty Dhyan power, and he will become Dhyan-deficient.

All of his imagination is based on his past impressions, lying in his subconscious mind. He projects these on the future to fulfil his cravings. So a person controlled by the mind always operates in the past and the future. This gives birth to a deficiency of Dhyan, that is, negative energy.

Now when a person gets connected to his soul or Dhyan, he lives in an abundance of Dhyan and sees a reality that is not distorted by his cravings or past impressions. He sees the red cloth for what it is.

The body and the mind are sources of stress, tension, fear, greed, attachment and all other negative energies. They keep you on the run at all times. They exhaust you to your limit. When you are completely exhausted, you awaken and find that you have wasted all your life running after the mind's desires, and gained nothing in return. Then you want to know where you have gone wrong. You search for the truth, and find that connecting with the self is the answer.

When you connect with yourself, you gain self-control. Your Dhyan level rises and you dispel the negative energy and rest in your being. You become peaceful and stable.

Big Bo tree

Bonsai Bo tree

When a person is connected to his soul and lives in abundance of Dhyan, he is like a big Bo tree under whose shade thousand peoples can rest.

When a person is running after the mind's desires and lives with a leakage of Dhyan, he is like a bonsai Bo tree, under whose shade nobody can rest.

Doing without Doership and Owning without Ownership is the Key

In the Bhagavat Gita, Shri Krishna said to Arjun, 'You are not a Doer. You are a medium through which actions are being done. Do what comes to you naturally, earnestly, without Doership.'

Why Are People Not Doers?

This is a crucial question. If one understands why he is not a Doer, his Doership drops. With this, all the negative energy related to doing will also drop, and he will become free from the stress, fear, tension and anxiety related to doing.

Now let us understand: what are the body and the mind, and what is soul or Dhyan? Our body and mind are inanimate matter just like any machine; let us say a washing machine. Our soul or Dhyan is positive energy like, for example, electricity. Without Dhyan, our body and mind are inanimate just like a washing machine without electricity.

We put clothes into the washing machine, connect it with the water supply, put in detergent and supply it with electric power. As we switch on the power supply, the machine washes the clothes. Who washes the clothes? The electricity is a non-Doer. It will power any machine that is connected to it. It can run the refrigerator, it can run the T.V., it can run the dishwasher, etc. The washing machine is designed to wash the clothes. So the washing machine is a Doer of action, and electricity is the non-Doer.

Similarly, our body and mind are matter, like the washing machine, and Doers of action, and our soul or Dhyan is the power that runs the body and mind and is a non-Doer. As we are not the body or the mind, but the soul, so we are non-Doers.

Shri Guru Arjun Dev Ji, in his *Bani Sukhmani Sahib*, says,

Jab Eah Janne Main Kichh Karta,
Tab Lag Gharab Juone Main Firta.

(When a person thinks of himself as a Doer, he continues to be recycled in new births.)

It is very important to know that non-Doership can sometimes be misunderstood as doing nothing. It is, in fact, doing everything with the perception that you are not a Doer, you are a medium through which action is being done.

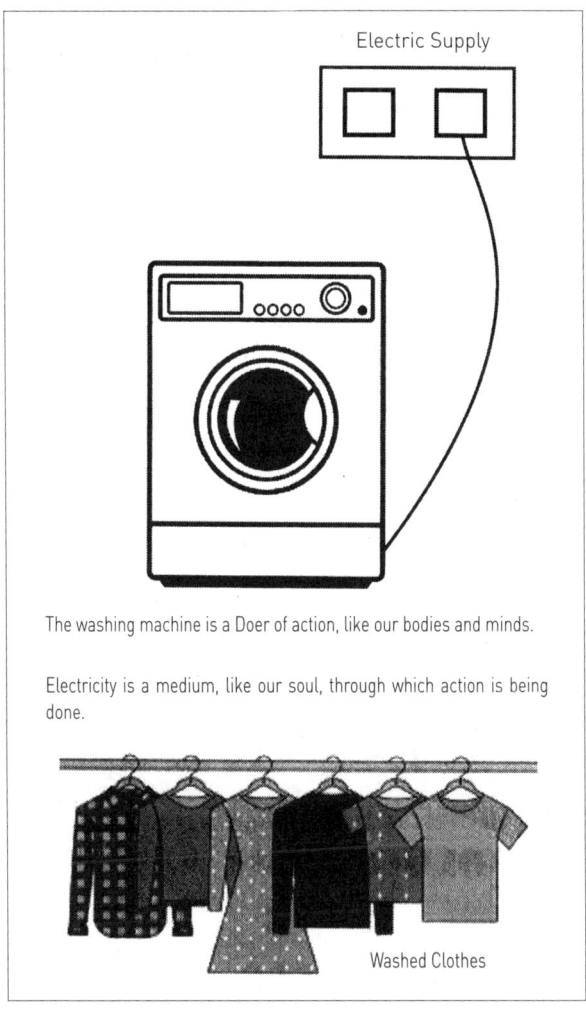

Electric Supply

The washing machine is a Doer of action, like our bodies and minds.

Electricity is a medium, like our soul, through which action is being done.

Washed Clothes

Ownership

Ownership binds you. You become a slave to what you own. If you own a beautiful house, you always worry for its maintenance, and if something happens to it you start worrying even more.

There is a beautiful story:

A cow owner was taking his cow to the village from the fields. The cow did not want to go to the village. The cow owner put a rope around its neck and was forcefully dragging it to the village.

Shaikh Farid, along with his disciples, happened to be passing that way. Farid saw the cow owner dragging his cow to the village. He asked the disciples to stop and learn a lesson. The cow owner also stopped to listen to Shaikh Farid.

Shaikh Farid asked the disciples one question:

'Between the cow and the cow owner, who is binding whom?' The disciples told Shaikh Farid that it was very clear that the cow owner was binding the cow, as the rope was tied around the neck of the cow and it was in the hands of the cow owner.

Now, Shaikh Farid asked the second question: 'What will happen when we cut the rope connecting the cow and the cow owner?' All the disciples started thinking; eventually they replied, that the cow would run away because it did not want to go to the village. Then the cow owner would have to run after the cow.

Shaikh Farid told his disciples that in the first instance, it looked as if the cow was bound by the cow owner, but in reality the cow owner was bound by the cow.

In conclusion, he said, 'Ownership binds you. If you own anything without ownership, it does not bind you. Your attachment with what you own gives you anxiety, and

Shaikh Farid and his disciples

Cow and Cow Owner

you become a slave of that which you own.'

Raja Janak told his disciples, 'I live in this magnificent palace, but this palace does not live within me. When I go out of this palace it does not bother me. If required, I can leave this palace right now without any remorse. This is the way of owning without ownership. If we own a thing without ownership, it does not worry us and we remain peaceful and free.'

Nature's Cycle and Cosmic Duality

A water drop formed from melted snow in the mountains falls into the river stream and travels thousands of kilometres to be one with the ocean. Similarly, a soul that has fallen into the river of the material world travels through thousands of lives to be one with the Creator. The last destination of every drop of water is the ocean, and the last destination of every soul is the Creator or the soul of the universe or super Dhyan. The ocean completes the journey of a water drop, and being one with the Creator completes the journey of every soul. Both the water drop and the soul have to continue their journeys till they reach their final destinations.

Everything in this universe is on its journey to the final destination. The more things reach their destination, the more other things set out on their own journeys, and the cycle of nature goes on.

The distance a water drop has to travel depends upon its place with respect to the ocean. A water drop closer to the ocean is likely to meet it sooner. Similarly, a soul having a higher Dhyan level has a greater chance of being one with the Creator.

The Train of Nature

Human is soul. This soul is journeying through the train of nature. His body and mind are nature. His self is travelling in the train of body and mind, which is called life. This train of nature is passing through different stations called birth, childhood, teenage, adulthood, old age and death.

This train of body and mind travels according to the laws of nature. It runs on its own speed as governed by nature. The soul has nothing to do with its governance. The human soul is like a passenger, it does not play any role in governing the train of body and mind.

Body and mind are mechanical things that run on their own. The human soul is merely a witness, like a passenger sitting in the coach of the train. If we recognize our soul and get connected to it and start experiencing it, we can enjoy the journey of our life, just like a passenger becomes comfortable after boarding the train and rests in his or her seat and enjoys the scenic beauty of nature through the window, while interacting with co-passengers.

Human Doership is akin to running inside a train compartment in the hope that this will somehow help you reach the destination faster. All this does is fill you up with tension, fear and stress, and spoil the charm of your journey. This is how Doership is spoiling your beautiful journey of life.

Cosmic Duality

There was a primordial field in the beginning, which

scientists call the unified field. We may call it the absolute. Then something happened, perhaps the Big Bang, and the unified field split up into relative fields or electromagnetic gravitational fields. The interplay of these fields gave birth to matter and energy, and the material world came into existence.

Our holy books say that there was only the absolute in the beginning; nothing else existed. The absolute wished the physical universe into existence. The Holy Bible says things happened after God wished them to.

With the split of the relative from the absolute, cosmic duality came into existence. One split into two is cosmic duality—we may call it the material world. For the material world to run, duality is necessary, just as two legs are required for walking.

What Is Cosmic Duality?

In the material world everything is in pairs, one opposite to the other. For example, Day and Night, Joy and Sorrow, Cruelty and compassion, Justice and Injustice, Animosity and Friendship, Good and Bad etc.

When your Dhyan level is raised, you realize all such things that seem opposite to each other are not, in fact, opposite—they are the extensions of each other, or, we may say, two faces of the same coin. For example, day cannot happen without night, joy cannot happen without sorrow, justice cannot happen without injustice, good cannot happen without bad, and so on.

In reality, they are not dual or two—they are extensions of each other—that is, continuous or one. When you realize they are one, you rise above the cosmic duality and achieve unity.

The Four Lawan of Sikh Marriage

ਸੂਹੀ ਮਹਲਾ ੪ ॥

ਹਰਿ ਪਹਿਲੜੀ ਲਾਵ ਪਰਵਿਰਤੀ ਕਰਮ ਦ੍ਰਿੜਾਇਆ ਬਲਿ ਰਾਮ ਜੀਉ ॥

ਬਾਣੀ ਬ੍ਰਹਮਾ ਵੇਦੁ ਧਰਮੁ ਦ੍ਰਿੜਹੁ ਪਾਪ ਤਜਾਇਆ ਬਲਿ ਰਾਮ ਜੀਉ ॥

ਧਰਮੁ ਦ੍ਰਿੜਹੁ ਹਰਿ ਨਾਮੁ ਧਿਆਵਹੁ ਸਿਮ੍ਰਿਤ ਨਾਮੁ ਦ੍ਰਿੜਾਇਆ ॥

ਸਤਿਗੁਰੁ ਗੁਰ ਪੂਰਾ ਆਰਾਧਹੁ ਸਭਿ ਕਿਲਵਿਖ ਪਾਪ ਗਵਾਇਆ ॥

ਸਹਜ ਅਨੰਦੁ ਹੋਆ ਵਡਭਾਗੀ ਮਨਿ ਹਰਿ ਹਰਿ ਮੀਠਾ ਲਾਇਆ ॥

ਜਨੁ ਕਹੈ ਨਾਨਕੁ ਲਾਵ ਪਹਿਲੀ ਆਰੰਭੁ ਕਾਜੁ ਰਚਾਇਆ ॥੧॥

ਹਰਿ ਦੂਜੜੀ ਲਾਵ ਸਤਿਗੁਰ ਪੁਰਖੁ ਮਿਲਾਇਆ ਬਲਿ ਰਾਮ ਜੀਉ ॥

ਨਿਰਭਉ ਭੈ ਮਨੁ ਹੋਇ ਹਉਮੈ ਮੈਲੁ ਗਵਾਇਆ ਬਲਿ ਰਾਮ ਜੀਉ ॥

ਨਿਰਮਲੁ ਭਉ ਪਾਇਆ ਹਰਿ ਗੁਣ ਗਾਇਆ ਹਰਿ ਵੇਖੈ ਰਾਮੁ ਹਦੂਰੇ ॥

ਹਰਿ ਆਤਮ ਰਾਮੁ ਪਸਾਰਿਆ ਸੁਆਮੀ ਸਰਬ ਰਹਿਆ ਭਰਪੂਰੇ ॥

ਅੰਤਰਿ ਬਾਹਰਿ ਹਰਿ ਪ੍ਰਭੁ ਏਕੋ ਮਿਲਿ ਹਰਿ ਜਨ ਮੰਗਲ ਗਾਏ ॥

ਜਨ ਨਾਨਕ ਦੂਜੀ ਲਾਵ ਚਲਾਈ ਅਨਹਦ ਸਬਦ ਵਜਾਏ ॥੨॥

ਹਰਿ ਤੀਜੜੀ ਲਾਵ ਮਨਿ ਚਾਉ ਭਇਆ ਬੈਰਾਗੀਆ ਬਲਿ ਰਾਮ ਜੀਉ ॥

ਸੰਤ ਜਨਾ ਹਰਿ ਮੇਲੁ ਹਰਿ ਪਾਇਆ ਵਡਭਾਗੀਆ ਬਲਿ ਰਾਮ ਜੀਉ ॥

ਨਿਰਮਲੁ ਹਰਿ ਪਾਇਆ ਹਰਿ ਗੁਣ ਗਾਇਆ ਮੁਖਿ ਬੋਲੀ ਹਰਿ ਬਾਣੀ ॥

ਸੰਤ ਜਨਾ ਵਡਭਾਗੀ ਪਾਇਆ ਹਰਿ ਕਥੀਐ ਅਕਥ ਕਹਾਣੀ ॥

ਹਿਰਦੈ ਹਰਿ ਹਰਿ ਹਰਿ ਧੁਨਿ ਉਪਜੀ ਹਰਿ ਜਪੀਐ ਮਸਤਕਿ ਭਾਗੁ ਜੀਉ ॥

ਜਨੁ ਨਾਨਕੁ ਬੋਲੇ ਤੀਜੀ ਲਾਵੈ ਹਰਿ ਉਪਜੈ ਮਨਿ ਬੈਰਾਗੁ ਜੀਉ ॥੩॥

ਹਰਿ ਚਉਥੜੀ ਲਾਵ ਮਨਿ ਸਹਜੁ ਭਇਆ ਹਰਿ ਪਾਇਆ ਬਲਿ ਰਾਮ ਜੀਉ॥

ਗੁਰਮੁਖਿ ਮਿਲਿਆ ਸੁਭਾਇ ਹਰਿ ਮਨਿ ਤਨਿ ਮੀਠਾ ਲਾਇਆ ਬਲਿ ਰਾਮ ਜੀਉ ॥

ਹਰਿ ਮੀਠਾ ਲਾਇਆ ਮੇਰੇ ਪ੍ਰਭ ਭਾਇਆ ਅਨਦਿਨੁ ਹਰਿ ਲਿਵ ਲਾਈ ॥

ਮਨ ਚਿੰਦਿਆ ਫਲੁ ਪਾਇਆ ਸੁਆਮੀ ਹਰਿ ਨਾਮਿ ਵਜੀ ਵਾਧਾਈ ॥

ਹਰਿ ਪ੍ਰਭਿ ਠਾਕੁਰਿ ਕਾਜੁ ਰਚਾਇਆ ਧਨ ਹਿਰਦੈ ਨਾਮਿ ਵਿਗਾਸੀ ॥

ਜਨੁ ਨਾਨਕੁ ਬੋਲੇ ਚਉਥੀ ਲਾਵੈ ਹਰਿ ਪਾਇਆ ਪ੍ਰਭੁ ਅਵਿਨਾਸੀ ॥੪॥੨॥

Shri Guru Ram Das ji, in his bani, explained the four stages required for a human to reach the Creator of the universe, called the four Lawan. This bani is used to solemnize the marriage of two souls. This means that the meeting of two souls is like the meeting of two drops of water, and the meeting of a soul and the Creator, or the soul of the universe, is like a drop of water meeting the ocean. Both of these involve four stages.

These four stages are:

1st Lawan: Satguru says Nature is responsible for human karmas. Negative karmas can be dissolved by adapting true humanism through reciting bani and experiencing one's soul, which vanishes all sorrows. The mind is purified and it comes to rest. With this, one is blessed and starts feeling Ananda. This is the beginning of the journey to meet the creator.

2nd Lawan: Satguru says that after the mind is purified, one is blessed enough to come in contact with a truly enlightened person, who guides one to be fearless and egoless. With this, one starts feeling the presence of the Creator of the universe all around, and in everything. One sees him in and out. In this stage, one starts listening to the cosmic sound, which is called Anhad Shabad.

3rd Stage: Satguru says that in this stage, one's mind starts feeling blessed and contented, which results in good fortune and meeting with holy people. With their help, the unknown is revealed and the continuous experience of the soul is started in one's heart. In the third stage one feels content, free and detached.

4th Stage: Satguru says that as the mind comes to rest after purification and the soul is experienced, this becomes an easy routine with His grace. As a result, the Creator of the universe is revealed. The experience of the soul leads one to Ananda. In the fourth stage, the soul is immersed in the soul of the universe.

Holy books say that the human body and mind are nature or Parvati, who is the bride, and Dhyan, or Shiv, who is the groom. The nature bride is sleeping and the Dhyan groom is always awake. The nature bride does not meet her groom, Dhyan, while she is sleeping. When she awakens, the bride and groom meet each other—which is called experiencing the soul or meditation. When we start experiencing our soul all the time—a state that the holy books call 'married forever'—we are ready to be immersed in the ocean of the Creator of the universe.

How to Raise Dhyan Level

Dhyan is our superpower. Every human being has his own Dhyan level. If our Dhyan level is low, we live a miserable life. We can become criminals easily if such a situation arises. We are always in conflict with others. We live in brutal ego. We are always in suspicion, fear, tension, stress and other negative energies. Low levels of Dhyan give birth to deficiency of Dhyan, or negative energy. We are in conflict with the universe and fight to be a separate, independent entity from the universe, which is never possible. This leads to a stressful and unhappy life.

When our Dhyan level is very high, we live a happy life. We are in harmony with the universe. We live comfortably with others. We remain egoless. Hence negative energy cannot form, as there is no leakage of Dhyan. We are always full of positive energy and compassionate to others. We live in oneness and enjoy our life.

Dhyan Level High

Real Human Being

Soul (Dhyan)

Fearlessness
Trust
Selflessness
Discipline
Peace
Responsibility
Innocence
Forgiveness
Non-Duality
Contentment
Truthfulness
Freedom
Wealth
Wisdom
Purity
Compassion
Health
Honesty
Non-Guilt
Happiness
Honour
Love
Faithfulness
Knowledge
Benevolence
Detachment
Dispassion
Beauty

All Positive Energy Original Human Nature Living in Present Main Cause: Non-Doership

When connected with the soul, the Dhyan level rises greatly.
One is filled with positive energy and godly powers

Dhyan Level Low

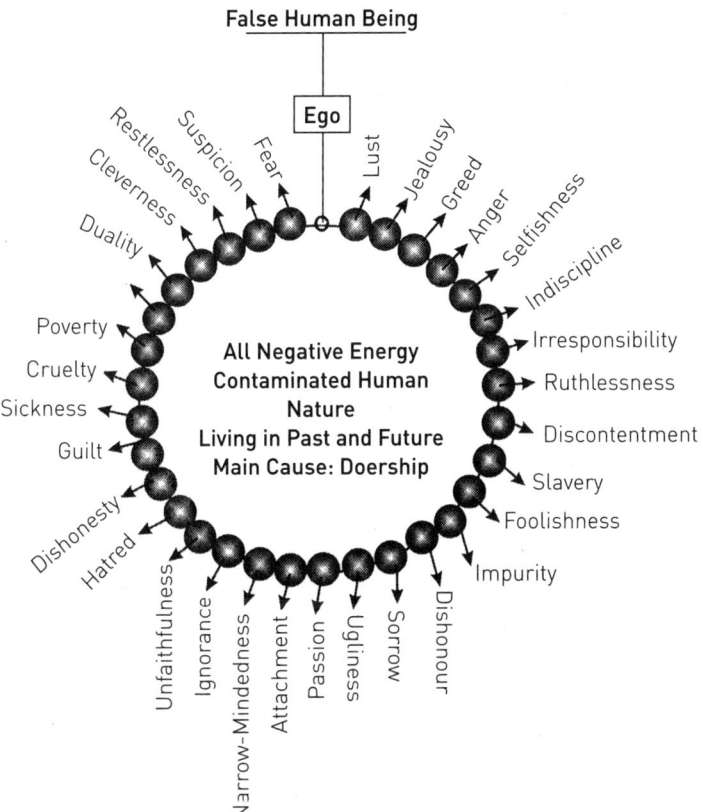

Due to disconnect from the soul and leakage of Dhyan, Dhyan level falls sharply. One is filled with negative energy and negative powers.

Comparison of Life with Low and High Dhyan Levels

Dhyan Level Low	Dhyan Level High
1. Living in joy, sorrow and bondage.	Living in Ananda, a stage beyond joy and sorrow.
2. Living in past and future.	Living in present.
3. Living in Doership, ownership and ego.	One is awakened and becomes egoless.
4. Running after mind without self-control.	Living in self-control.

5.	Gets easily disturbed.	Always at peace and stable.
6.	Dhyan is divided in many directions.	Dhyan is united.
7.	One leads stale life goes on repeating things again and again from the past.	One leads a constantly fresh and new life.
8.	One's breath goes shallow and erratic results in to the malfunction of vital organs.	One's breath goes deep and smooth resulting in healthy organs and good health.
9.	It leads to a stressful and discontented life.	It leads to a peaceful and contented life.
10.	One's heart is filled with hatred and the mind is closed.	One's heart is filled with love and the mind is open.
11.	One emits negative energy.	One emits positive energy.
12.	One is always in conflict with others and feels separate from the universe.	One is always in harmony with others and feels oneness with the universe.
13.	Running after material possessions, status and physical pleasures.	Always content with what one has and living in peace and Ananda.
14.	One invites bad fortune.	One is blessed and invites good fortune.
15.	One ends up wasting their whole life and gets ready to be born again.	One enjoys life to the fullest, contentment and then transcends it forever.

How to raise Dhyan level?

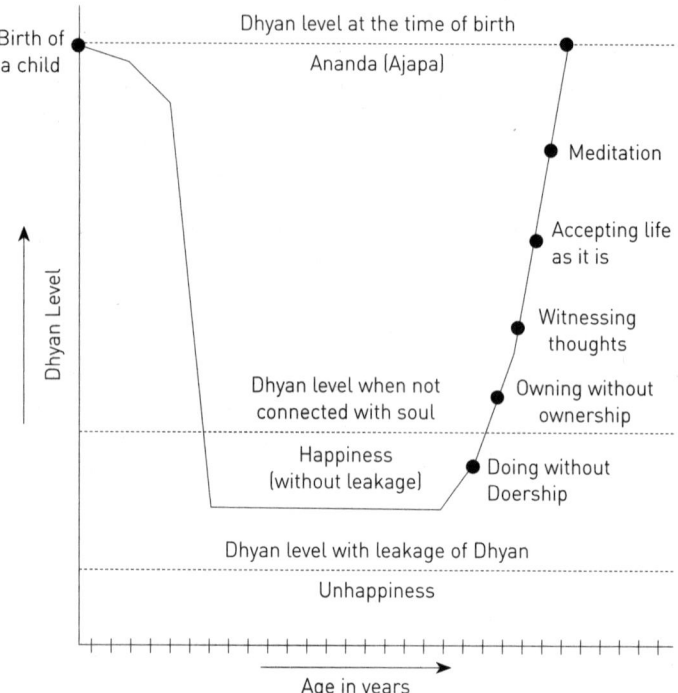

Dhyan level drops drastically after teenage. It can be raised by doing without Doership, owning without ownership, witnessing thoughts, accepting life as it is and meditation.

What Zarathushtra and Guru Nanak Taught Humankind

'Think good, feel good and do good,' said Zarathustra. When we think good, feel good and do good, there is no leakage of Dhyan and there remains no scope of formation of negative energy. So we lead an optimal life.

Guru Nanak in his Bani's First Pauri of Japuji Sahib says,

ਸੋਚੈ ਸੋਚਿ ਨ ਹੋਵਈ ਜੇ ਸੋਚੀ ਲਖ ਵਾਰ ।

ਚੁਪੈ ਚੁਪ ਨ ਹੋਵਈ ਜੇ ਲਾਇ ਰਹਾ ਲਿਵ ਤਾਰ ।

ਭੁਖਿਆ ਭੁਖ ਨ ਉਤਰੀ ਜੇ ਬੰਨਾ ਪੁਰੀਆ ਭਾਰ ।

ਸਹਸ ਸਿਆਣਪਾ ਲਖ ਹੋਹਿ ਤ ਇਕ ਨ ਚਲੈ ਨਾਲਿ ।

ਕਿਵ ਸਚਿਆਰਾ ਹੋਇਐ ਕਿਵ ਕੂੜੈ ਤੁਟੈ ਪਾਲਿ ।

ਹੁਕਮ ਰਜਾਈ ਚਲਣਾ ਨਾਨਕ ਲਿਖਿਆ ਨਾਲ ।

(Your thinking is limited; you cannot know Him even if you may think of Him lakhs of times. You cannot achieve silence inside even if you sit in meditation [as your mind is mechanical and it does not stop its babble]. Your hunger cannot die even if you have loads of delicious food. Your wisdom may be multiplied by a lakh, but it cannot carry you beyond material world. Now Satguru asks: How to be a true human being? And how to break the shackles of this false material world? Now, he himself answers his questions:

He says that we can do so by obeying our Creator, by accepting life as it naturally comes to us, by being content in our selves, our being and our humankind.)

He says, 'Accept your life as blessed by the creator and be content in yourself.'

Living in Present

Human beings are born to live in the present. When he is born, a person is in the present. The 'present' is optimum living, as life is always fresh and new in the present. In the present, you are at complete rest; you are in your original nature, all your senses are free, and you are a complete human being. In the present there is no mind, no distractions and no leakage of Dhyan—this is why you always remain connected to yourself.

In the present you are one with the Creator and you become peaceful and stable and go beyond joy, sorrow and bondage or the material world. You become one with the universe and settle in oneness and unconditional manifestation.

In the present, your Dhyan level is very high and there is no scope for the formation of negative energy—you always live in positive energy. You become a source of positive energy. It is a blissful stage where you transcend karmas. At this stage, no karmas form because Dhyan does not flow into the subconscious mind, and all past impressions lying in the subconscious mind dry out for want of Dhyan Power, just as a green crop dries out without water.

In the present, you enjoy the best of both worlds. You enjoy the material world and ultimately transcend it to join the Creator of the universe.

We are not able to live in the present because we are not connected to ourselves. We are operating through our mind, which is a source of distraction that operates through the subconscious mind. Past impressions lying in the subconscious mind or memory push our mind towards material pleasures. So we live a life of joy, sorrow and bondage. This is a life of misery, as our Dhyan Power leaks and we become weaker and weaker.

The past impressions actively affect us as the Dhyan Power flows through the subconscious mind, making our past karmas grow, flower, and bear fruit. We then reap them like crops. The mind always operates in the past and the future, and keeps draining Dhyan Power. In the present there is no mind, no leakage of Dhyan and no karmas.

In order to be in the present we need to connect to our self. We must observe non-Doership and non-ownership; we must witness our thoughts and we must accept our life as it naturally comes to us. Then we enter the deep meditation stage where we start remaining connected to our self at all times. This stage is called 'Ajapa'. It is a stage of continuous recitation. Then we are able to live in the present. In the present, we are simultaneously in the past, present and future. We feel blessed all the time.

When you are at complete rest, it is Dhyan and you are

divine. Complete rest means not thinking, feeling or doing, which further means doing without effort or non-Doership. This state of complete rest is also called the 'present'. You are not able to stay in the present due to the conditioning of the mind. Only a high level of Dhyan can decondition it. If you want to remain in the present, then raising your Dhyan level is the only solution.

The Great Master Lautzu

After struggling for many years, Lautzu could still not find peace. He was desperate and had abandoned all hope. One day, he was sitting under a tree, exhausted, when he saw a dry leaf fall to the ground. He saw that as soon as the leaf touched the ground, the wind blew it back up to the sky. Yet again the leaf fell on the ground, and was again moved by the wind in the opposite direction. Lautzu kept looking at the leaf.

There, he became absorbed in thinking, 'What if I become like this dry leaf and surrender to the cosmic power and go where it takes me, with no choice of mine?'

He became enlightened and a blessed person.

You are perfect. You are self-sufficient. Your head is right where it should be. You are alone by nature. You are pure by nature. You are free by nature. You are not a Doer, so you are not responsible for karmas. You are not the owner of anything. You are beyond birth and death. You are an almighty soul. Stay where you are, as you are. Do not run. This running depletes your mighty Dhyan

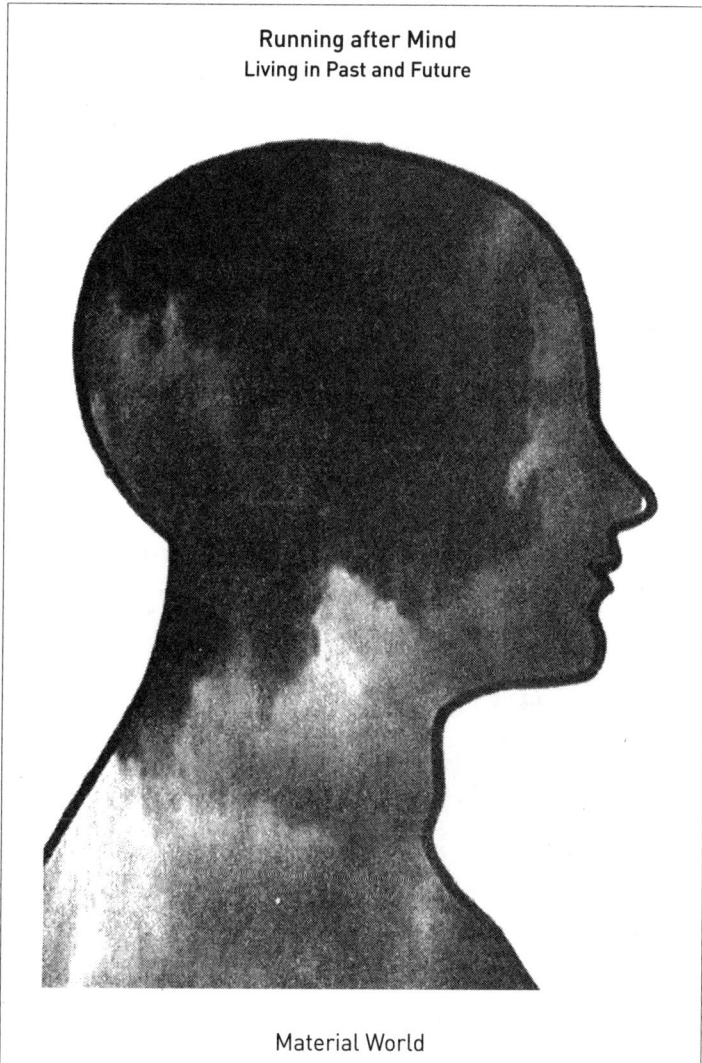

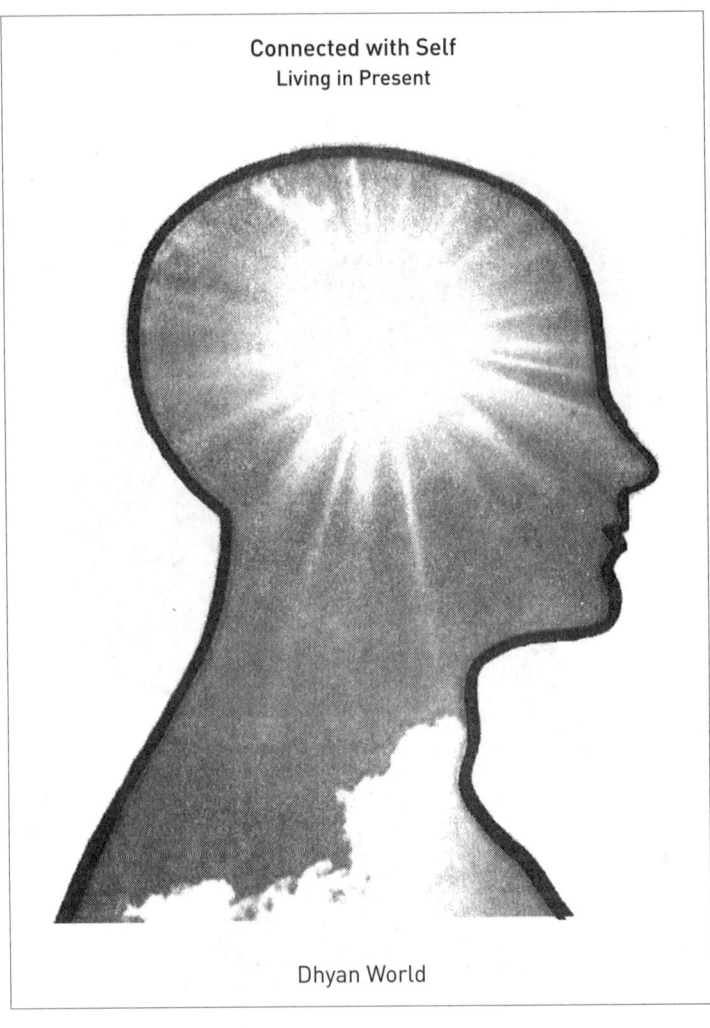

Connected with Self
Living in Present

Dhyan World

power, making your life miserable. Remain connected to yourself to be in your true nature, present, peace and Ananda forever.

PART-3

YOU ARE THE ONE
YOU ARE LOOKING FOR

Introduction

A most funny thing has happened to this planet Earth. God has forgotten himself. He has built so many places to search for him in. He has written countless books to know him through. He worked hard and designed painful austerities to reach him through.

An even funnier thing is that he cannot find his 'self' till he is visiting these places, reading books and performing austerities. Because he resides in the Doer, not the doing.

Now he needs another God to tell him that he is God and to make him believe that his 'self' is God. Because his 'self' is the whole universe itself.

The very day God comes to know his 'self', the restlessness in this world will be over. Harmony and peace will prevail, and planet Earth will become the house of Gods.

The Dhyan World

What is Dhyan?

Dhyan is also known as soul, consciousness, awareness, attention, and the soul of universe. Dhyan and the universe are one and the same. Dhyan means 'alertness'. The greater your Dhyan, the more alert you are and the longer you stay young. The universe itself is Dhyan. Its Dhyan level is very high, beyond all limits. So it is most alert. Even the smallest particle cannot escape its attention. As a result, it will forever remain young.

The largest living beings, like whales in the ocean or elephants on earth, and the smallest ones, which cannot be seen with a naked eye—such as bacteria or germs—all have soul, Dhyan or consciousness. At the level of Dhyan, there are no distinctions. Human beings are also Dhyan, soul or consciousness. Never can they escape Dhyan.

As space and consciousness are the same thing and neither has borders, everything in the whole universe falls within this. Everything takes birth from this, is sustained by this for life, and absorbed back into this after life. So everything in the universe belongs to consciousness or Dhyan or soul. Dhyan is everything—there is nothing without Dhyan. Even 'nothing' is Dhyan. Across the world this Dhyan, consciousness or soul is represented through countless names that vary with geography, culture, time and society.

Among all living beings, only humans have the most valuable opportunity to become one with Super Dhyan while alive, because only the human mind is conscious. No other living beings have this opportunity, as their minds are not conscious. Only the conscious mind can receive Dhyan from Super Dhyan and raise the Dhyan level high enough to become one with Super Dhyan while living.

Dhyan is beyond description, as it is beyond attributes. You cannot describe it. There is no language that can express it. But you can still know it. Because you can 'be' Dhyan. You are already 'him' but you have forgotten your 'self', which is 'him'. To experience 'him' or your 'self' you need someone who has already experienced his 'self'. He will connect you with your 'self', which is Super Dhyan itself. You can then experience it. When you experience it, you come to know that you can 'become' him but cannot express him.

Dhyan World

The whole universe comprises the Dhyan World. It is the real world. It is always at complete rest. It is constant, it is pure, omnipresent, omniscient, and omnipotent. It is eternal. All the powers lie in the Dhyan World. The material World also runs on the power of Dhyan.

The material world in the universe is like waves on the surface of the ocean. These waves are on the surface of the ocean, but beneath them, the entire ocean is at rest. Similarly the matter world is just on the surface of the universe, and beneath it, the Dhyan world is always at complete rest. That is why when we come to rest from within, we get connected to Dhyan World and become powerful.

Why Do You Suffer When You Go Against Your Consciousness?

The whole universe is a soul or consciousness. Since a human being is also a soul, we can say he is the whole universe. When a person goes against his consciousness he goes against the whole universe—in other words, he is turning his back on the supreme power, the Creator and Sustainer of the universe. As a result, he misses the presence of his Creator and so his Dhyan level goes down. With this new deficiency of Dhyan, negative energy takes over, giving birth to suffering. In other words, the whole universe goes against him, which is why he suffers.

What Happens When You Become a Doer?

Humans are souls, not bodies and minds. The soul is a positive energy or power through which action is being done. That is why the soul is a non-Doer. As humans are souls, they are also non-Doers. When a human perceives himself as a Doer he is going against his consciousness and turning his back on his Creator, which breeds a deficiency of Dhyan resulting in restlessness, tension, stress, fear and all manner of negative energies—ultimately bringing misfortune and suffering.

Similarly, ownership, cravings and bad thoughts are products of the mechanical mind that compels you to go against your consciousness and turn your back on the Creator, thus dragging you into misfortune and suffering.

When we become aware that we should not act against our consciousness and start abiding by it, we save a lot of positive energy or Dhyan, and our Dhyan level rises greatly. We start living in an abundance of Dhyan. We live in peace and Ananda, which is our true nature.

Matter World

This matter world in which we live is not separate from the Dhyan World, just as waves of the ocean are not separate from the ocean. The matter world is the reflection of the Dhyan world—its shadow, in other words.

In the Gita, Shri Krishna says the matter world is just like the reflection of a tree in a calm pond.

In order to free your Dhyan from the material world you will have to cut the root of this tree with the axe of renunciation or detachment. You cannot free your Dhyan by plucking its leaves one by one or cutting its branches. Because the more you cut, the more new leaves and branches will emerge.

The Water Pond

The material world lies in your cravings. You are not satisfied with what you have—you wish to have more. You want to change your life again and again. Even change will not satisfy you.

Stop running after change. Be satisfied with what you

have and settle down in contentment. Say, 'What I have, is more than enough. I don't need anything more and I do not want to change anything. My life is wonderful as it is.' Then you will have cut to the root of the matter while living in the material world. And so, you will have freed your Dhyan from the material world while living in it.

There is nothing wrong with the material world. It is a part of the Dhyan world itself, just as the waves of the ocean are not separate from the ocean. It is your cravings, your running after change, that is bad. Because of these, you leak your mighty Dhyan power and that makes you miserable.

If you settle down in contentment without cravings, you become very powerful because all the leakage of your Dhyan power is stopped. Then, your wishes are automatically fulfiled without any effort—perhaps without you even needing to make the wishes. The things you had been running after start running after you. You lead a contented life with your Dhyan power, united in peace and Ananda.

The material world is a reflection or shadow of the real Dhyan world. It is not real, just as your shadow is not real. It cannot exist without the Dhyan world, just as your shadow cannot exist without you. The Dhyan world is the real world because it can exist without the material world.

Doership is like trying to catch your shadow and govern its movements. It is not possible. But if you simply govern your body's movements, your shadow will automatically be governed.

Similarly, if you want to govern the material world, then govern the Dhyan world. The material world will automatically be governed.

There is a beautiful story: A renowned saint was passing through a street in a town. All of a sudden, he heard a child crying bitterly inside a house, and stopped in

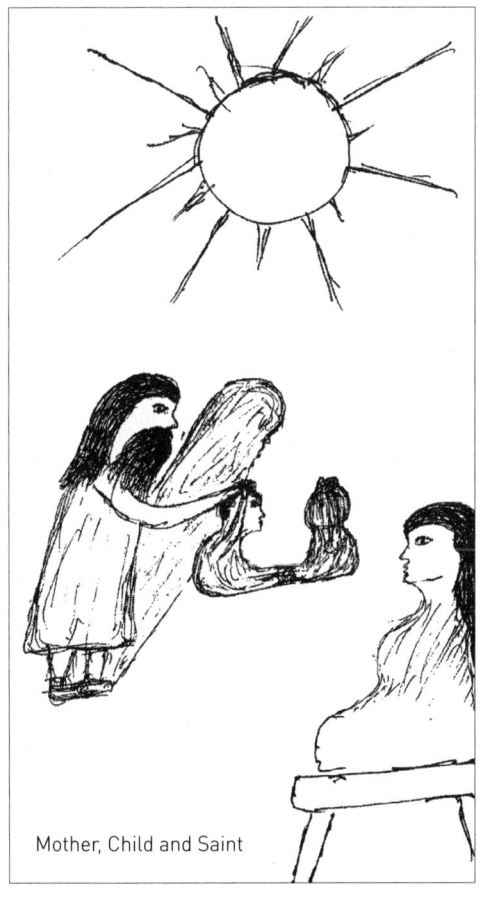

Mother, Child and Saint

front of it. The door was open and he looked inside it, to find a mother and a little child relaxing in the winter sun in their courtyard. The little child was trying to catch his shadow, taking it to be a toy. The more he tried to catch it, the more it escaped, and the child continued to try in vain until he got exhausted and started crying. The mother tried to pacify him by telling him that the shadow could not be caught, but it was beyond the child's understanding and his crying grew even louder.

The saint watched the whole episode and understood the problem. He entered the house, took the child's tiny hands, and placed them on his head. The child, seeing his shadow, began to think that he had finally caught the shadow by the head. The child jumped with joy and started laughing loudly instead of crying. The mother also started laughing.

The saint thanked the child for teaching him a great lesson: If you want to handle the shadow, you handle the thing that produces the shadow.

The Three Planes of Existence and Freedom

Human life on earth can be divided into three planes.

1. SOLID PLANE: Anything we can touch, see or sense with our physical senses can be called solid material. All solid materials exist in the solid plane. Our body is also solid material. Solid materials have gravity which keeps them grounded on Earth.

2. SUBTLE PLANE: The subtle plane lies between the Earth and the sky. All subtle materials lie in this plane. For example, oxygen gas lies in this plane. Oxygen is subtle material as it cannot be touched or sensed with physical senses but has nevertheless been proven to exist materially. Oxygen has gravity, so it exists in the air, near the Earth. The higher up we go, the lower the quantity of oxygen in the air. It becomes difficult to breath on the mountains because of the lower quantity of oxygen. Eventually, if we move up high enough, we run out of oxygen.

Similarly, our mind is also subtle material as we cannot

touch or sense it physically. Anything coming from our mind, such as desires, feelings, thoughts, likes and dislikes, is also subtle material. These materials remain near the surface of the Earth in the subtle plane, because they also have gravity.

Once a person breaths his last, his body, which is solid material, is dropped or eliminated and Dhyan carries a bag of subtle material, such as desires, with it and floats in the subtle plane. This becomes the reason for rebirth. Unsatisfied desire is carried by Dhyan or the 'Creator' to a mother's womb to for rebirth. Dhyan, entangled in the subtle materials, cannot free itself to reach the casual plane; it keeps on floating until it enters the mother's womb according to the unfulfilled desire.

3. CASUAL PLANE: The casual plane lies above the solid and subtle planes. It is purely in the Dhyan World. No material, solid or subtle, can reach it. The casual plane is free from the gravity of the material world. This is purely a world of pure consciousness where Dhyan, freed from the material world, can reach.

When a person frees his Dhyan from the material world while alive, it can reach the casual plane to merge with the Super Dhyan or the Creator of the universe. This is possible when a person is able to raise his Dhyan level high enough to drop all the desires, feelings, attachments and the duality of the material world. When he breathes his last, he merges with the Creator of the whole universe.

Freedom

Every human being wants freedom, because freedom is his true nature. When he is free, there is no leakage of Dhyan, and Dhyan power flows freely. When Dhyan power flows freely there is no suffering, because all of the person's senses are free (as Dhyan is not stuck anywhere). Then, he is in his true nature, 'Ananda', as he was right after birth.

The main problem with human beings is that they only know about physical freedom, not internal freedom. But his true freedom lies not in physical freedom but in internal freedom. 'Internal freedom' is the freedom of his Dhyan from past impressions lying is his subconscious mind. He may achieve physical freedom, but he keeps on living as a slave of his subconscious mind and continues suffering. When he is able to come out of his subconscious mind, only then does real freedom prevail for him. At that point, even physical slavery cannot cause him suffering.

Complete physical freedom is not possible, because the entire world is interdependent. Every moment, we are dependent on the universe. Dependence means slavery. We need to live in oneness and harmony with others. This is only possible when we are internally free. So, real freedom lies in freeing your Dhyan power from the subconscious mind. Then, your Dhyan does not dissipate in memory but remains in present—that is to say, your true nature, freedom or Ananda.

Source of Happiness

When your happiness depends upon something else—some relation or some cause—you cannot be forever happy. Your happiness will be temporary, because everything in the material world changes with time. If you want to be happy forever, then connect with your soul and raise your Dhyan level. When you live in an abundance of Dhyan, you will be happy and satisfied with what you have in your life and every change that your life goes through. You will remain happy always in every situation and live an optimum life.

Settle Inside Yourself

We try to change the world outside. Our focus is thus on the outside. It is very difficult to change the world outside unless you are settled in peace inside yourself. If you are, then everything outside will start falling in place.

Your material world lies in the restlessness within you, not outside. If you take care of your restlessness and settle in peace, then everything around you will settle automatically. As soon as you settle in peace inside, the outside world stops affecting you. Things become more disturbed when you get affected by them. Your reaction to the situation is the most important factor that determines its outcome. If your reaction is peaceful, things get settled quickly and the outcome will be positive.

The Spring of Happiness Lies within You

The spring of happiness lies in your true self, within you. Material gravity is the major obstruction that clouds the spring of happiness. The only way to clear the obstruction of material gravity is to raise your Dhyan level. When your Dhyan level reaches 'Ajapa' or 'Auto-Recitation', you go beyond material gravity and start floating in the present. It is the ultimate spring of happiness, and it is eternal.

Faith, Destiny, and the Two Types of 'I Am'

Two Types of 'I am'

People live in two types of 'I am'. One is false, and the other is real. All the problems and suffering of human life are due to the false 'I am', as he forgets the real 'I am' due to distractions of mind.

Birth of the False 'I am'

A human being is soul or Dhyan or the real 'I am'. His original nature is Ananda. His body and mind are natural and part of the material world. They are not his original nature. His mind is an instrument between his body and his soul. Originally, the mind is pure and peaceful. It is an instrument to receive Dhyan from Super Dhyan. Dhyan keeps the mind running, but when Dhyan gets entangled in the mind, the mind starts perceiving itself as the Creator (since Dhyan is the Creator of the universe). This gives birth to false 'I am' or Doership.

The material world is not bad in itself. The mind is also not bad in itself, and neither is Dhyan. But the entanglement of Dhyan in the mind or the material world is bad. Because it is the source of the false 'I am' or Doership, which causes leakage of the mighty Dhyan Power and thus becomes the cause of human suffering.

So to be happy and peaceful, our primary job is to withdraw our Dhyan from the mind and rest it in our soul. When we withdraw our Dhyan from the body and the mind and rest in our soul, we live in an abundance of Dhyan, which is real freedom.

Human Life Is the Real 'I am'

Human suffering is because of his false 'I am'. Human beings are always trying to come out of this false 'I am' by doing selfless service, visiting holy places, reading holy books or surrendering to a deity. By doing so, his false 'I am' gets dropped or surrendered and he gets connected to the real 'I am', which is his soul. But such service, holy places or deities play no actual role in his surrender of the false 'I am'. He can surrender it wherever he is, whenever he wants, without them. But he does not know this. His belief that he has disconnected himself from the false 'I am' through service, etc. gives him happiness, and he is filled with positive energy. This flow of positive energy raises his Dhyan level, which further neutralizes negative energy. He feels relieved and becomes happy.

But this relief is temporary. For permanent relief, you need to get directly connected to your soul. If you experience your soul on a daily basis, your Dhyan level goes on increasing slowly, until you enter the stage of 'Ajapa' or Auto-recitation. Then your contact with your soul continues forever and you become a source of positive energy. You enter your true nature, Ananda.

Faith Is Amrit

Having deep Faith in your soul is the key to Ananda. Your deep faith in your soul or the Creator takes you beyond the material world and you become peaceful. Deep faith is Amrit (nectar), which gives you real life. Have faith, do not have attachment. Faith belongs to the soul and attachment belongs to the mind. Faith raises your Dhyan level and strengthens you, while attachment leaks your Dhyan and weakens you.

You draw energy from the object of your faith. If you have faith in another person, then you can draw a very small amount of energy, according to their level of Dhyan. If you have deep faith in the Creator of the universe or your soul, you can draw a tremendous amount of energy, as the Creator has unlimited energy. The energy you receive depends on the intensity of the faith you have in that object and the level of energy it contains. If you have very high intensity faith in the Creator of the universe, you can receive unlimited energy from it.

Doubt Is Poison

Doubt is a creation of the mind. The mind is the source of all negative energy. The mind is mechanical. It wants to protect you by doubting everybody and everything. In this process, it forgets peaceful living. All these doubts are mechanical and imaginary, arising from a deficiency of Dhyan. So they eat away all of your positive energy and make you suffer. So it is better to evaluate a risk than to doubt.

Faith is real—it belongs to the soul. It is the source of positive energy. That is why it is called Amrit (nectar). Faith strengthens you. It makes you fearless. It makes you think positive thoughts. It carries you to optimum living.

If you make an earnest effort to raise your Dhyan level and simultaneously live in doubt, the effects of the rise in Dhyan level will be nullified. The positive energy of Dhyan will be eaten away by the negative energy produced by the doubts. So it is most important to have deep faith in yourself when you make an effort to raise your Dhyan level, so you can experience the full effect of the positive energy in your life.

Your doubts are the main source of your restlessness and worries. These change your behavior towards other people, giving rise to strained relations.

Destiny

Our bodies, minds and intellects are mechanical—they operate like any other machine. They work under the principles of 'cause and effect', which we call karmas. Let us take the example of a car. 'Water leakage' from the radiator of a car becomes the 'cause' producing the 'effect' of the engine overheating and breaking down. Similarly, eating too much sugar for too long becomes the 'cause' that produces the effect of 'diabetes' in a person. If we install software in the car to detect the cause at the beginning, we can spare ourselves the effect and save money, time and effort. Similarly, if a human connects with his self and gets self-control over the mind, he can restrict his mind from overindulging in sugar at the beginning to avert the 'effect' of diabetic sickness, saving money, time and effort and staying healthy.

When you are running after the mind, you are unconsciously creating your destiny, which is the outcome of the past impressions lying in the subconscious mind— of which you are not aware. When you make efforts to raise your Dhyan level, you attain self-control, transcend the body and mind and come to know that you are responsible for your own karmas and destiny. Now you can easily witness the traits of the mind and start operating consciously to remake your destiny. When you further grow in Dhyan level you move into 'Ajapa' or auto-recitation, which permanently connects you to your soul. Then you become the master of your destiny. Your mind becomes 'no mind'. You start operating in the universal mind, which works spontaneously. You come to rest from within and settle in peace and Ananda, which is your true nature. Then everything happens by itself and does not form any karmas. It is perfect and spontaneous.

The Body, the Mind, and Dhyan Leakage Control

Human Body and Mind

A bubble is formed on the surface of a river when wind carries water from a wave. The bubble appears on the surface of the water and has a different shape and properties from its basic constituent elements, air and water. When the bubble bursts, water goes back to water and air goes back to air.

Similarly, our physical body is formed by five elements—Earth, Water, Air, Fire and Space. When a human being breaths his last, these five elements go back to themselves. Earth goes back to earth, water goes back to water, air goes back to air, fire goes back to fire and space goes back to space. If Dhyan is free from the material world, then even Dhyan goes back to Super Dhyan.

Surface tension between water molecules is the cause of the formation of bubbles on the surface of water. Similarly,

Dhyan power retention in the subtle material of a desire is the main cause of the formation of human bodies in the material world.

Without Dhyan power, the human body is not much different from the body of a car. Both are products of the Earth. Both run on the food from the Earth. Both bear name plates for identification. Both are run by Dhyan power. In both cases, their constituent elements go back to the basic elements for recycling after life.

The Two Types of Power: Physical and Cosmic

Physical power belongs to the material world. Physical power is produced from the food we eat. Food also belongs to the material world. The food we eat is digested through the natural physical system and physical energy is gained. Our physical enjoyment also depends on our level of physical energy. But we cannot enjoy physical pleasure without self-control, which comes after we connect to our self.

Dhyan energy or cosmic power is gained through our Dhyan level. This Dhyan energy brings self-control and neutralizes the negative energy produced in the human mind by negative thoughts or actions. When the level of Dhyan is high, there remains no negative energy in the human mind and the use of physical energy is optimum. When this happens, a person lives in peace and Ananda with a high level of physical energy, which is called optimum living.

How to Escape Dhyan Leakage

All human senses are sources of leakage of the super power of Dhyan. The human body has ten senses. To live in the material world, these ten senses are very important. For optimum living, we need to live with all the senses always free.

Our mind receives Dhyan from Super Dhyan and supplies it to the bodily senses to run them. This is a natural system of working and living in this material world. Our problem occurs when our Dhyan gets stuck in some sense organ and Dhyan leakage starts. We keep thinking about that sense for an inordinate period of time and waste our Dhyan power.

Three of these senses (speaking, hearing and seeing) consume 75 per cent of our Dhyan energy in normal life. To come out of Dhyan leakage, we need to take care of these three senses first.

Control over these senses can be initiated by living alone for five to six days. This will ensure that the wastage of Dhyan energy in speaking, listening and seeing is controlled, and at the same time, direct our Dhyan power inward rather than outward. Our Dhyan is continuously flowing outward, which is a major reason for the leakage of Dhyan. We need to turn the flow of Dhyan inward, which is first step to connecting with our soul.

When you live alone there is not much incentive to speak, listen and see. You save a lot of Dhyan energy, which enhances your Dhyan level, with the result that your happiness level is increased.

However, when you live alone, a dialogue still continues inside you—between your mind and intellect. They are like two different people sitting inside you and interacting with each other. This interaction between the mind—or more accurately, the subconscious mind—and the intellect is mechanical. It has nothing to do with your soul. Mind and intellect are purely mechanical things. You cannot stop their dialogue. But when your Dhyan level is raised, their dialogue decreases. It takes a long time to come to an end.

Then, with practice, your Dhyan leakage comes under control and you turn inward. Now you are ready to connect with your soul, or for meditation. You are ready to raise your Dhyan level by observing the following rules:

1. Doing without Doership
2. Owning without ownership
3. Witnessing your thoughts
4. Accepting life as it comes to you
5. Meditation

How to Be Peaceful

Raja Janak explained to his Guru Ashtavakra, 'Now I have come to know that the winds of thoughts and imagination emanating from my mind are causing ripples on the surface of the still pool of my consciousness. They originate by themselves and end by themselves. Neither can I create them, nor can I stop them, as they are natural processes in my mind. My attachment to them takes me to a mixture of joy, sorrow and bondage which gives birth to restlessness. However, detachment from them takes me to a peace which I can simply achieve by becoming a witness and not involving myself with them. They will then start by themselves and end by themselves, without affecting me. I will remain peaceful.'

A High Level of Dhyan Keeps You Young

The human body comes from Dhyan. It is being run by Dhyan. So Dhyan is the energy on which human health is dependent. When a person lives in an abundance of Dhyan, he remains healthy. When he lives with a deficiency of Dhyan, his health is affected. All his sicknesses are products of his deficiency of Dhyan. In other words, when he operates through the subconscious mind he operates with a deficiency of Dhyan and becomes addicted. He lives a stale life, as he gets filled up with all the negative energy. He lives in stress, fear and doubt. All his organs are under stress, which breeds sickness. To live a healthy life, he should live in abundance of Dhyan. Dhyan is alertness. The greater your Dhyan level, the more alert you are. The greater your alertness, the more you stay healthy and young.

Brutal Doership

The basic problem of human beings is that they suffer from Doership. Doership leaks a person's super power of Dhyan and makes him powerless and miserable. All negativity in the world, like terrorism, oppression, cruelty and crime, happens because of Doership. Doership is very difficult to understand, because we have concentrated our Dhyan power on Doership or 'I am' for such a long time that we have become hardcore Doers. It is our false addiction to Doership that now it has become difficult to understand and accept that we are not doers.

When we make an effort to do anything, we are under the spell of Doership. Our true nature is non-Doership. When we are non-doers, we need not make any effort to do anything. We may call it 'effortless effort'. In our true nature, everything becomes effortless, because we are full of Divine power, being connected with our soul or the Creator of the universe. All of our senses are free to act. In this stage, we are peaceful, powerful and alert.

In short, running is Doership. When we stop running we come out of the spell of Doership. There is a beautiful story that illustrates this:

Buddha was travelling with his monks. On the way, he saw a dense forest. He asked his monks to stop, as he wished to enter the jungle alone. The monks immediately began dissuading him, as the jungle was known to be home

to the dreaded criminal known as Unglimal. It was believed in the surrounding villages that no stranger entering the forest would come back out alive, as Unglimal would kill them with an axe, then proceed to chop off their fingers and wear them around his neck. Thus the name Unglimal—which means 'necklace of fingers'.

Buddha asked them not to worry and assured them that he would come back safe. He entered the jungle alone. Deep inside, he heard footsteps and realized that someone was following him. It was Unglimal, who was running after Buddha to catch him. But no matter how fast he ran, he could not catch up with him. When he ran out of breath, he said loudly, 'Oh monk, stop!' Hearing his voice, Buddha stopped, faced Unglimal and said, 'I stopped long ago. When will you?'

Hearing these magical words from Buddha's mouth and seeing his radiant face, Unglimal could not utter a word in reply. His inner being felt a shock of divine grace and he threw away his axe, along with his necklace, and fell at the Buddha's feet. He murmured, 'Master, forgive me and accept me as your disciple.'

Buddha asked Unglimal to get up and follow him. They emerged from the jungle together, shocking the monks. Unable to think past their hatred and fear, the monks stayed away from Unglimal.

Unglimal started living with Buddha's monks, but they never accepted him. After a long time, he complained to Buddha that his monks still hated him and that he felt that they would never accept him. Buddha told him to stay patient. His heap of karmas being huge and hard to dissolve, it would take time.

Unglimal followed Buddha's words and became a noble man. Eventually, all his karmas got dissolved. He became a great midwife, helping women deliver children and comforting them as they did so. Owing to his past experiences, he was never affected by the cries of the mother delivering the child.

Unglimal got transformed and became a great, noble soul.

Brutal Doership is very hard to dissolve. Only a great saint with a very high Dhyan level like Buddha can help one dissolve it.

Guru Nanak, Bala and Mardana were travelling when they came across an inn and a house. As the sun was setting and night approached, they stopped for food and rest at the inn. A man with clean clothes and a sweet voice came to them and urged them to have food and rest in his house. Guru Nanak asked him his name, to which he replied that his name was Sajjan (which means 'friend'). Guru Nanak accepted his invitation. He served them well and gave them bedding to rest at night.

Guru Nanak stayed awake till late into the night. He saw Sajjan returning again and again to ask them to sleep. Guru Nanak could sense trouble. He asked Mardana to ready his Rabab (a musical instrument), as he wanted to sing a divine song.

In the song, the Guru sang in a clear voice that a man will have to face the truth after his life. He will have to account for all his karmas and will be punished for his bad karmas.

Listening to the song, sung in such clear words, and seeing the divine radiance on the face of Guru Nanak, Sajjan's brutal Doership melted away. His inner being was shaken badly by his erstwhile criminal intent. Sajjan threw himself at the feet of Guru Nanak and asked for repentance. Guru Nanak asked him to rise and admit to the crime.

Sajjan told Guru Nanak that he used to kill strangers in their sleep, rob them of their belongings and throw the corpses into a well deep inside the jungle.

Guru Nanak asked him to bring everything he had robbed from the strangers. Once Sajjan did so, the Guru asked him to distribute them to needy people in the name of the Divine One. Sajjan followed the instructions of the Guru without delay. Now Guru Nanak accepted him as his disciple and connected him with the Divine Name (that is, his soul) and asked him to meditate and serve the people in the area.

Dreaded criminals are the products of brutal Doership. It drains Dhyan power to the extent that a person becomes a devil. This is the lowest level of Dhyan, below which a person can commit suicide. When such a person meets a person with a very high Dhyan level, such as Buddha or Guru Nanak, his negative energy cannot withstand the higher level of positive energy in front of it and starts crumbling. Finding a source of positive energy, his soul awakens. In this situation, the person has no option but to surrender before the saint, in order to unburden his

self of negative energy and brutal Doership. Then the overinflated balloon of brutal Doership bursts and the process of transformation is initiated. The person realizes his folly and completely turns his life around, eventually becoming a noble soul.

From Ananda to Suffering, and Back to Ananda

Human is Ananda. His true nature is Anand Sarup. His true nature is Dhyan. Dhyan is Anand Sarup. When he lives in an abundance of Dhyan and his Dhyan flow is free from the entanglement of the material world, he lives a life in Ananda. People are connected to their souls at birth, and live in an abundance of Dhyan as children. So they are always in Ananda. As children start growing, so do their minds, which begin distracting them. Their Dhyan starts leaking and their Dhyan levels start falling. Now they become entangled in the material world in hopes of drawing Ananda from it, which is not possible. The more entangled a person gets in the material world, the more he leaks his Dhyan Power and the more his Dhyan level drops. This happens because he gets disconnected from his soul. In normal course, after teenage, Dhyan level drops drastically due to the distractions of the mind.

As an adult, physical energy is predominant and a person needs a partner to enter the reproductive cycle of nature. He gets married, produces children. Then he also enters a profession to earn a livelihood. Now he has to pay attention to his wife, his children, and his ageing parents alongside other social responsibilities. He becomes hugely burdened. Modern day technologies like mobile phones, WhatsApp, internet, Facebook and TV have added to his woes. He has no time to think for himself. His mind runs in many directions, dividing his Dhyan power endlessly, which results in heavy leakage of Dhyan. This heavy leakage gives birth to restlessness, suffering and broken relations. He becomes a most dissatisfied person. Now he searches for an effective way to come out of this mess of a life and be happy.

How He Can Begin to Raise His Dhyan Level

To come out from this mess of a life, raising your Dhyan level back to what it used to be is the only solution.

Kundalini or Serpent Energy

'Serpent energy' is the energy that connects a human being to cosmic energy or Super Dhyan Power. When the Dhyan of a human being flows through the lower three energy centers of his body (Root, Sex and Navel), this energy lies at the lower end of the spinal cord, unaffected. It can be compared to a serpent sleeping with its body coiled up and its head down. This indicates that the human is living his life in a dream or in his subconscious mind. When we awaken this serpent energy by performing breathing exercises, it raises its head just like a snake and begins moving upward. It connects a human being with cosmic power through the seventh energy center, the crown chakra. After this connection is established, the person is awakened and comes out of the dream world of the subconscious mind.

The metaphor of 'serpent energy' represents the 'alertness' of human beings. When a person is connected to cosmic power or super Dhyan, he is most alert. Dhyan is alertness. The greater your Dhyan level, the more alert you are.

How to Meditate

With breathing exercises, we can awaken our kundalini or serpent energy and cleanse our mind simultaneously. A cleansed mind comes to rest. With awakened kundalini and a mind at rest, we immediately get connected to our soul, or Anhad Shabad.

Our mind is directly influenced by our breathing. When we are angry, our breathing runs faster than when we are calm. Taking advantage of this factor, we can empty our mind temporarily with breathing exercises. Our empty mind comes to rest and we easily get connected to our soul. The human body has seven energy centres. To cleanse the mind properly, we must divide them into three parts and exhale our breath with a little force from these places:

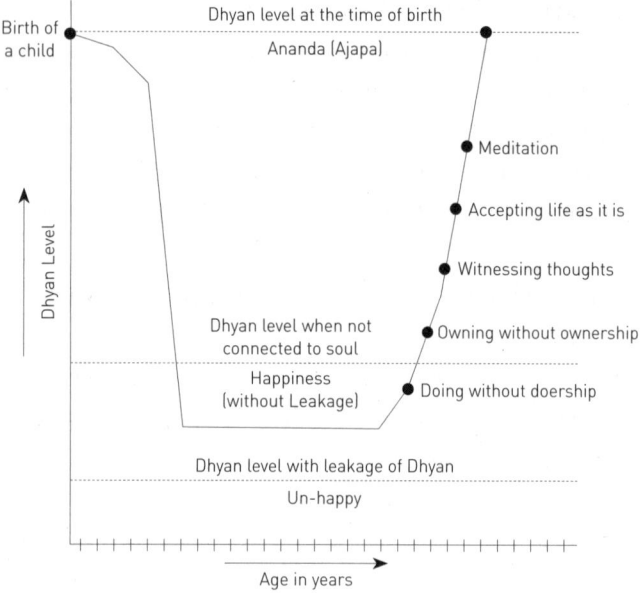

Dhyan level drops drastically after teenage. It can be raised by doing without doership, owning without ownership, witnessing thoughts, accepting life as it is and meditation.

(a) The first place is between lowest end of the spine and the navel.

(b) The second place is between the heart and the navel.

(c) The third place is slightly above the forehead.

This process must be repeated forty to fifty times, in the order of a>b>c. Take the help of an experienced person for this.

By performing this breathing exercise, our empty, restful mind can get connected to Anhad Shabad, or our souls.

Try to listen to the cosmic sound, which various saints have described differently according to their experiences. Kabir compared it with the sound of the rain. Other saints have compared it variously with the sound of wind, that of beetles, and that of musical instruments like the flute or ringing bells.

For an elaborate explanation of Anhad Shabad, refer to Stage 1 of the book.

Ajapa, or Unconditional Manifestation

The entire universe is an unconditional manifestation. It is running without an effort. Plants are growing, flowering and bearing fruits without any effort. Birds are chirping, flying, making their nests and laying eggs without any effort. Animals are grazing, hunting, mating and living without any effort. Rivers are flowing thousands of kilometers to reach the ocean without any effort. The sun and moon are rising and setting daily, ever since their inception, without any effort. All the planets, stars and galaxies are moving without any effort.

When you become a non-Doer, your work becomes effortless. You do everything, but without any effort or exertion. You do it in Ananda. You do it while resting inside, with all your senses free. This is called 'effortless effort'. When you undertake 'effortless effort', you become blessed and fortunate. You live a peaceful and happy life. This 'effortless effort' is possible when you enter 'Ajapa' or continuous recitation. It is unconditional manifestation.

Ajapa or Continuous Meditation or Auto-recitation

'Ajapa' or continuous recitation is the stage of your Dhyan level where you enter the Dhyan world after neutralizing the gravity of the material world. After this, you lead your life as per your routine. You go to work, you eat, you sleep, you gossip with your friends, you interact with your family as usual—but this continuous recitation or Ajapa or continuous meditation continues without break, by itself, inside you. You always remain peaceful and centered.

This represents non-Doership, which means that while doing everything, you are doing nothing, as everything is effortless. You are not making any effort. In Ajapa, you transcend space and time. Now regardless of where you are in the world, or the time, your stability and peace are not affected.

Living in Ajapa is a most pious stage. It means that while living in the material world, you have achieved victory over it. There is no formation of karmas, as you do not need to make any effort to do anything—it happens naturally. Dhyan power does not flow into the subconscious mind. So all the past impressions lying in the subconscious mind dry out for want of Dhyan power, just as green crops dry out for want of water. New karmas do not form, as there is no leakage of Dhyan and everything is done with 100 per cent Dhyan. As there is no leakage, therefore no addiction is formed. So you live a fresh and new life forever.

In Ajapa, you are connected to your soul all the time so you become a non-Doer even as you do everything.

It means that you are going to many places, but are not going anywhere. You eat everything, yet you have not eaten anything. You do all your work, but you have not done anything. You speak a lot, but you have not spoken at all. It is because you have dropped Doership. It is your 'Doership' or ego or false 'I am' that does everything and becomes a Doer. As soon as you enter Ajapa, your Doership or ego or false 'I am' comes to an end, and you become a soul and a non-Doer. Everything then happens naturally by itself in unconditional manifestation.

In Ajapa, you go beyond space and time, which means you go beyond body and mind or nature, which further means you go beyond the material world. That is why you are able to live in the present in peace and Ananda forever. At this stage, there are no karmas and there is no death.

A Beautiful Story

Queen Rukmini appealed to Shri Krishna, 'Darwasa Rishi has come to our place. He is meditating across the Yamuna river in the forest. We should offer him food and take his blessings.' Shri Krishna agreed and asked her to do the needful.

Rukmini prepared a vast amount of delicious food, suitable for all tastes, and asked her friends to come along, carrying the food in stuffed containers along with fruits and sweets. But the Yamuna was overflowing, and Rukmini asked Shri Krishna how they could cross it.

Shri Krishna told her to go to Yamuna and appeal to

her, 'If the Rishi has never eaten any food, please help us cross your waters.' They did so, and Yamuna lowered her waters and allowed them to cross. Once they reached the Rishi and shared the food, he was happy and blessed them. As he talked to them, he finished all the food. Now they took the Rishi's blessings for the return journey, but Rukmini looked anxious. Seeing this, the Rishi asked her what was wrong. She replied, 'While coming here, we followed Shri Krishna's advice and asked Yamuna, 'If the Rishi has never eaten any food, please help us cross your waters,' and Yamuna conceded. But we forgot to ask Shri Krishna how to get back.' The Rishi told her to make the same request. They all felt confused, but there was no other alternative. They did so, and Yamuna once again lowered her waters and allowed them to cross.

Confounded, they went to Shri Krishna for the mystery's solution. Shri Krishna told them, 'The Rishi has never eaten any food, and will never do so, because he is in 'Ajapa'. He is a soul—he is no longer a body and a mind. Food can only be eaten by the body, not the soul. In Ajapa, even as you do everything, you do nothing.'

Shri Guru Gobind Singh in his bani says to yogis:

ਆਤਮ ਉਪਦੇਸ਼ ਭੇਸੁ ਸੰਜਮ ਕੋ ਜਾਪੁ ਸੁ ਅਜਪਾ ਜਾਧੇ ॥
ਸਦਾ ਰਹੈ ਕੰਚਨ ਸੀ ਕਾਯਾ ਕਾਲ ਨ ਕਬਹੂੰ ਬਯਾਧੇ ॥੩॥੨॥

(Preach connecting to the soul and restraint of mind. Remain in 'Ajapa' or auto recitation. Then your body and mind will remain light and shining like gold. You will transcend time and become deathless.)

Life Is a Film Displayed on the Screen of Space and Time

Human life is a most beautiful gift that we have received from the universe. We can enjoy it to the fullest if we know where we are going wrong. We have taken birth in such a beautiful planet, Earth—all green forests, blue oceans, rivers, mountains, deserts, and plain fertile land. It has so many beautiful countries with a wide variety of people. We have made so many scientific discoveries, making human life easier. We have formed beautiful human relations that allow us to have all manner of feelings and sentiments. We have achieved good governance and better systems of living.

By all accounts, we should be living in Heaven. But we have spoiled all this by perceiving a false 'I am'. We have wrongly identified this body and mind as 'I am'. This body and mind is not you. This is a temporary gift from the universe. You can enjoy it by dropping false 'I am' and connecting with the real self or real 'I am', which is your soul, and living in an abundance of Dhyan. Then you can use this gift of body and mind to your contentment.

When you drop your false 'I am' or Doership or ego, you become soul. Your soul and the soul of the whole universe are the same—which means that you are the whole universe. Your soul is a witness. Now you can witness the whole universe. When you become your real self, you live in peace and Ananda forever.

The real task is to free your Dhyan from the material world and make all your senses free. When all your senses are free, you become a witness or soul.

Master Dogen says, 'Stop following words and letters. Learn to withdraw your Dhyan from the mind and reflect it on yourself. If you do so, your body and mind will naturally fall away and your original Buddha nature will appear.'

In the Gita, Shri Krishna says, 'Withdraw your Dhyan from everything and reflect it on me (your soul).'

If your Dhyan is stuck anywhere then you cannot be free and you cannot enjoy your optimal life. If your Dhyan is free and you are living in 'Ajapa' then you come to know that it is unconditional manifestation. Things are happening by themselves as per the wishes of the Creator of the universe.

The Creator of the universe is Dhyan itself. When you leak your dhyan you leak the Creator of the universe. You leak your super power. You become cursed and weaker and thus you suffer. When you gain Dhyan power, you gain the Creator of the universe and become blessed, powerful and happy. Your self is Him. If you gain Him you become blessed, powerful and feel Ananda. If you lose Him you become cursed, powerless and miserable.

Guru Nanak says he is all in all. He is one in all and all in one. Everything and every living being depends upon him.

ਹੁਕਮੀ ਹੋਵਨਿ ਆਕਾਰ
ਹੁਕਮੁ ਨ ਕਹਿਆ ਜਾਈ ॥
ਹੁਕਮੀ ਹੋਵਨਿ ਜੀਅ
ਹੁਕਮਿ ਮਿਲੈ ਵਡਿਆਈ ॥
ਹੁਕਮੀ ਉਤਮੁ ਨੀਚੁ
ਹੁਕਮਿ ਲਿਖਿ ਦੁਖ ਸੁਖ ਪਾਈਅਹਿ ॥
ਇਕਨਾ ਹੁਕਮੀ ਬਖਸੀਸ
ਇਕਿ ਹੁਕਮੀ ਸਦਾ ਭਵਾਈਅਹਿ ॥
ਹੁਕਮੈ ਅੰਦਰਿ ਸਭੁ ਕੋ
ਬਾਹਰਿ ਹੁਕਮ ਨ ਕੋਇ ॥

ਨਾਨਕ ਹੁਕਮੈ ਜੇ ਬੁਝੈ
ਤ ਹਉਮੈ ਕਹੈ ਨ ਕੋਇ ॥ ੨॥

The Guru says, 'The Creator or Dhyan is the maker of the material world. He cannot be expressed in words. He is the maker of all living beings and He is the cause of all respect.

He is the reason one moves into either misery or Ananda. He is the reason behind suffering and happiness. He is the reason behind the blessing and the curse. He is the cause of everything and every being—there is nothing outside him.'

The third Sikh Guru Shri Guru Amardas Ji in his Bani says,

ਪਉੜੀ ॥

ਆਪੇ ਧਰਤੀ ਆਪੇ ਹੈ ਰਾਹਕੁ ਆਪਿ ਜੰਮਾਇ ਪੀਸਾਵੈ ॥

ਆਪਿ ਪਕਾਵੈ ਆਪਿ ਭਾਂਡੇ ਦੇਇ ਪਰੋਸੈ ਆਪੇ ਹੀ ਬਹਿ ਖਾਵੈ॥

ਆਪੇ ਜਲੁ ਆਪੇ ਦੇ ਛਿੰਗਾ ਆਪੇ ਚੁਲੀ ਭਰਾਵੈ॥

ਆਪੇ ਸੰਗਤਿ ਸਦਿ ਬਹਾਲੈ ਅਪੇ ਵਿਦਾ ਕਰਾਵੈ॥

ਜਿਸ ਨੋ ਕਿਰਪਾਲੁ ਹੋਵੈ ਹਰਿ ਆਪੇ ਤਿਸ ਨੋ ਹੁਕਮ ਮਨਾਵੈ ॥੬॥

(The creator or Dhyan is the Earth Himself, He is Himself the farmer; He Himself sows the crop and He Himself grinds the flour. He Himself cooks and serves food in a plate, and He Himself eats it. He Himself is the water with which He Himself washes his hands; He is Himself the toothpick with which He cleans his teeth. He Himself calls the congregation and he Himself calls it off. He who blesses himself, comes to know about Him. Satguru says that the Creator or Dhyan is all Himself, in everything and every being.)

In his Bani Bhagat, Namdev Ji says:

ਪੰਨਾ 988

ਮਾਲੀ ਗਉੜਾ ਬਾਣੀ

ਭਗਤ ਨਾਮਦੇਵ ਜੀ ਕੀ

ੴ ਸਤਿਗੁਰ ਪ੍ਰਸਾਦਿ॥

ਧਨਿ ਧੰਨਿ ਓ ਰਾਮ ਬੇਨੁ ਬਾਜੈ॥

ਮਧੁਰ ਮਧੁਰ ਧੁਨਿ ਅਨਹਤ ਗਾਜੈ॥੧॥

ਰਹਾਉ॥

ਧਨਿ ਧਨਿ ਮੇਘਾ ਰੋਮਾਵਲੀ॥

ਧਨਿ ਧਨਿ ਕ੍ਰਿਸਨ ਓਢੈ ਕਾਂਬਲੀ॥੧॥

ਧਨਿ ਧਨਿ ਤੂ ਮਾਤਾ ਦੇਵਕੀ॥

ਜਿਹ ਗ੍ਰਿਹ ਰਮਈਆ ਕਵਲਾਪਤੀ॥੨॥

ਧਨਿ ਧਨਿ ਬਨ ਖੰਡ ਬਿੰਦ੍ਰਾਬਨਾ॥

ਜਹ ਖੇਲੈ ਸ੍ਰੀ ਨਾਰਾਇਨਾ॥੩॥

ਬੇਨੁ ਬਜਾਵੈ ਗੋਧਨੁ ਚਰੈ॥

ਨਾਮੇ ਕਾ ਸੁਆਮੀ ਆਨਦ ਕਰੈ॥੪॥੧॥

(With the Creator's blessings the sweet cosmic music "Anhad Shabad" happens without any musical instrument. With His blessings, it sounds like rain. With His blessings, Dhyan or the Creator Himself wears the dress of the human body. With His blessings, Mother Earth has received the Creator Himself in form of her child. He has blessed all the plants, the living spaces and the forests where the Creator himself is playing. He says, as the sweet music of his flute plays, the whole universe lives, and He Himself rests in Ananda.)

Answers to Three Questions

1. What is the truth and why?
    Human 'Self' (infinite consciousness) is the only truth.
    Because it existed in the beginning, it is existing now
    and it will continue to exist forever.
2. What is un-truth and why?
    Except human 'Self' (infinite consciousness), everything
    is un-truth. Because everything that we can perceive
    with our ten senses, ages. Everything takes birth, lives
    for a lifetime and then dies. A thing which was not once
    in existence but then came into existence and after will
    not exist after some time, cannot be truth.
3. What is human suffering and why?
    Human suffering is the deficiency of the energy of
    self or infinite consciousness. Because, the deficiency
    of superpower or the energy of self gives birth to
    restlessness or suffering, just like deficiency of light
    gives birth to darkness.

So, living in constant self-awareness is the solution to
human suffering.

Our mind is a wicked chaser. It keeps on chasing
our feelings and thoughts for nothing. It is like pushing
against a wall around the clock. In this process, it drains
our most precious energy of self or Dhyan. This is human
suffering or restlessness. If we witness this chasing of our
mind, this chasing stops. Our mind becomes relaxed. It
comes to rest and the pushing against a wall stops. Now

the mind is empty. The empty mind starts getting filled with the energy of self or Dhyan automatically, because this energy of self is always there around us in abundance. So a mind filled with this energy of self becomes the source of positive energy and we come out of suffering and become happy and blessed.

Just witnessing without getting involved is the way to live in present. You can do everything in life without getting involved or without pushing against a wall or being at rest from within. When you are not involved, you are a non-doer or you are a witness or you are in the present or you are the one you are searching for.

What Happens when Your Dhyan Level Rises?

HUMAN MIRROR
Human

Mind	Self
False I Am (Ego or Devil)	Real I Am (Egolessness or God)
100%	0%
90%	10%
50%	50%
10%	90%
0%	100%

Human beings who want to live stress-free, peaceful lives can raise their Dhyan (Awareness) level to wash off their false identity or false 'I am', to be in harmony and oneness with the universe—which is present and eternal.

The following is a beautiful story narrated by Swami Vivekananda:

Shortly after birth, a lion cub slipped and fell into a deep valley in the mountains. He was noticed by a shepherd boy. He picked him up and nursed him back to health. The cub survived and began growing. He started moving around with the herd of sheep and learning their habits. He learnt to walk like a sheep, cry like a sheep, move in tightly knit groups like the sheep, and be afraid of predators like the sheep. Very soon, he grew into a tall and beautiful lion that could be easily spotted among the sheep.

One day, a hungry old lion attacked the herd, which had strayed too close, but was surprised to see a young lion grazing among them. The older lion forgot his hunger and chased after the younger one. Not being accustomed to a lion's pace, the younger lion was easily caught. The old lion caught him by the scruff of his neck and dragged him to a pond to show him his reflection in the water. The young lion, seeing his own face alongside that of the old lion reflected in the water, was shocked. This shock brought him back to his innate nature as a lion and all of a sudden a roar broke out of his mouth and shook the whole valley.

This story is a metaphor for a human child being brought up in this material world just to survive. In the process, he forgets his innate nature and learns the false 'I am' that pushes him into the whole negative energy cycle, to live like sheep—full of fear, restlessness, anxiety and stress. He needs an experienced man who is established in his self, like the old lion, to show him his real face. At present he is being controlled by his body, mind and memory, which are mere instruments. After seeing his real face, he will come to know that his self is infinite consciousness and the controller of the whole universe. Then he will be able to regain control over his body, mind and memory, and live in peace and Ananda like a fearless lion.

Glossary

1. **Advaita:** Non-dual OR without duality OR unique.
2. **Ajapa:** Continuous auto-recitation OR continuous, endless meditation.
3. **Amrit:** Nectar that gives you eternal life.
4. **Ananda:** Eternal bliss OR a stage beyond joy and sorrow OR a stage of complete rest from within OR a condition of full development from within
5. **Ananda Swarup:** Eternal peace OR bliss.
6. **Anhad Shabd:** An automatic, non-instrumental sound that is unending and knows no limits OR the voice of silence OR the cosmic sound OR the vibration of infinite consciousness.
7. **Atma:** Soul OR self OR infinite consciousness.
8. **Bhagavat Gita:** One of the holy books of Hinduism. It contains teachings said to have come from Lord Krishna. The Gita is a doctrine of universal truth.
9. **Dhyan:** Infinite consciousness OR self OR soul OR awareness.
10. **Ganga:** A holy river.

11. **Karma:** Cause and effect OR impressions lying in the subconscious mind.
12. **Mala:** A string of beads or knots used in praying.
13. **Parvati:** Nature OR the material world OR that which is relative.
14. **Sansa:** False.
15. **Sansar:** The material world OR the restlessness of a human being.
16. **Sehaj:** Eternal peace OR eternal joy.
17. **Sehaj Smadhi:** Effortless meditation.
18. **Shiva:** Infinite consciousness OR universal soul OR the Absolute.
19. **Sukham:** Inner peace OR inner joy.